Accent on Meter

Accent on Meter

A Handbook for Readers of Poetry

Joseph Powell
Central Washington University

Mark Halperin
Central Washington University

National Council of Teachers of English
1111 W. Kenyon Road, Urbana, Illinois 61801-1096

For permission credits, see Permission Acknowledgments on page v.

Manuscript Editor: Lee Erwin
Production Editor: Bonny Graham
Interior Design: Doug Burnett
Cover Design: Evelyn C. Shapiro

NCTE Stock Number: 31468

It is the policy of NCTE in its journals and other publications to provide a forum for the open discussion of ideas concerning the content and the teaching of English and the language arts. Publicity accorded to any particular point of view does not imply endorsement by the Executive Committee, the Board of Directors, or the membership at large, except in announcements of policy, where such endorsement is clearly specified.

Library of Congress Cataloging-in-Publication Data

Powell, Joseph, 1952–
    Accent on meter : a handbook for readers of poetry / Joseph Powell, Mark Halperin.
        p. cm.
    Includes bibliographical references and index.
    ISBN 0-8141-3146-8 (pbk.)
    1. English language—Versification—Handbooks, manuals, etc.
2. English language—Rhythm—Handbooks, manuals, etc. 3. Poetry—Handbooks, manuals, etc. I. Halperin, Mark, 1940– II. Title.
    PE1505.P69 2004
    821.009—dc22
                                                              2004002930

Permission Acknowledgments

Bishop, Elizabeth: "One Art" from *The Complete Poems: 1927–1979*, by Elizabeth Bishop. Copyright © 1979, 1983 by Alice Helen Methfessel. Reprinted by permission of Farrar, Straus and Giroux, LLC.

Bogan, Louise: "Juan's Song" from *The Blue Estuaries*, by Louise Bogan. Copyright © 1968 by Louise Bogan. Copyright renewed 1996 by Ruth Limmer. Reprinted by permission of Farrar, Straus and Giroux, LLC.

Brooks, Gwendolyn: Excerpt—7 lines of "The Anniad," from the volume, *Blacks*. Reprinted by Consent of Brooks Permissions.

Collier, Michael: "Ghazal" from *The Ledge*, by Michael Collier. Copyright © 2000 by Michael Collier. Reprinted by permission of Houghton Mifflin Company. All rights reserved.

Cullen, Countee: "Incident," from *Color*. Copyright © 1925 by Harper & Brothers; copyright renewed 1953 by Ida M. Cullen.

Dickinson, Emily: poem #341, "After great pain, a formal feeling comes." Reprinted by permission of the publishers and the Trustees of Amherst College from *The Complete Poems of Emily Dickinson*, Thomas H. Johnson, ed., Cambridge, Mass.: The Belknap Press of Harvard University Press, Copyright © 1951, 1955, 1979 by the President and Fellows of Harvard College.

Frost, Robert: "Acquainted with the Night," "Design," "Nothing Gold Can Stay," and "Once by the Pacific," from *The Poetry of Robert Frost*. Edited by Edward Connery Lathem, Copyright © 1928, 1969 by Henry Holt and Co. Copyright © 1936, 1956 by Robert Frost. Copyright © 1964 by Lesley Frost Ballantine. Reprinted by permission of Henry Holt and Company, LLC.

Gunn, Thom: "Rastignac at 45" from *Collected Poems*, by Thom Gunn. Copyright © 1994 by Thom Gunn. Reprinted by permission of Farrar, Straus and Giroux, LLC.

Hamill, Sam, translation of "Elegy" by Yuan Chen, from *Crossing the Yellow River: Three Hundred Poems from the Chinese* (BOA Editions, 2000).

Halperin, Mark: "Resolve" and "The Alarm" from *Backroads*. Reprinted by permission of Pittsburgh University Press and the author. "Mists and Imagined Fields," from *The Measure of Islands*. Reprinted by permission of Wesleyan University Press and the author.

Housman, A. E.: "With Rue My Heart Is Laden," from "A Shropshire Lad: Authorized Edition," from *Collected Poems of A. E. Housman*, © 1965 by Henry Holt and Company. Reprinted by permission of Henry Holt & Co., LCC.

liam Carlos Williams. Reprinted by permission of New Directions Publishing Corp.

Yeats, W. B.: "Adam's Curse" and "An Irish Airman Foresees His Death." Reprinted with the permission of Scribner, an imprint of Simon & Schuster Adult Publishing Group, from *The Collected Works of W. B. Yeats, Volume I: The Poems.* Revised, edited by Richard J. Finneran. (New York: Scribner, 1997).

Every effort has been made to identify the holder of copyright for the adaptation of a Martial epigram on page 152, which was attributed to "T.M.W." and published in *Latin Poetry in Verse Translation, from the Beginning to the Renaissance,* edited by L. R. Lind (Boston: Houghton-Mifflin, 1957). Under "Notes" in that volume appears the following: "All versions signed T.W.M., G.I.C., or W. F. Gosling are from the pages of *Greece and Rome,* I–IV (1931–35) and IX–X (1939–41)." No volume with that title appears in Lind's bibliography.

Contents

Acknowledgments

We wish to thank Central Washington University for its generous support of our work. Additional thanks are due to those at NCTE, particularly Lee Erwin, for her superb editing skills; Bonny Graham, for her expert guidance of the project through production; and Kurt Austin, for his faith in the project. Finally, we would like to thank our students who have helped shape and clarify this book over the last four years. Their successes and suggestions encouraged us to present it to a wider audience.

Preface

We have been teaching a Poetry and Poetics class for a number of years and have been dissatisfied with the anthologies aimed at introducing poetry to students. The "poetics" sections are always inadequate. Students typically have problems with hearing the meter in poems, and yet receive almost no guidance in chapters on meter. On the other hand, books about meter are too technical for students who know nothing about it. It was the need to find something in between that encouraged us to put a book together ourselves. We wanted a book that would give a detailed analysis of the metrics in a number of poems, so that students could practice and test themselves. The primary impulse behind this book was to provide students with ample opportunities to learn how to **scan**. (Note: words and phrases in bold typeface are defined in the glossaries, and appear in the index, which will lead the reader to the sections where they are treated in detail.) We also wanted to make a few remarks on the process of scansion and the importance of meter to the poems themselves.

There are a number of philosophies regarding **scansion**. These philosophies derive, in part, from ideas about stress. Our approach is to emphasize simplicity. At the heart of traditional **meter** is a basic regularity, which gives the metrical poem its distinctive sound. Departures from this regularity provide a mechanism for emphasis. Robert Frost once wrote that there are two methods for writing metrically in English: strict iambs and loose iambs (see his "The Figure a Poem Makes"). He meant that the trochee is merely the foot in an iambic line that starts differently, and that the other feet are used primarily for variations or substitutions to give the iambic line more range. For him, strict iambs implied a classical sense of regularity, a cadence that dominated the poem; loose iambs could imitate speech more closely and allowed a broader variety of tones.

We view stress as a binary quality. A syllable is either stressed or unstressed. We recognize that some stresses differ qualitatively from others. A word like "strength" differs greatly from a word like "to," but in the stress environment of the poem, both can be stressed. Light syllables, like short prepositions, can get metrical stresses. But they nonetheless become part of the basic pulse of the poem. Other writers have distinguished four levels of stress and have been concerned about metrical boundaries in ways that lead to far more complex treatments than the one we followed. We acknowledge that there are other ways to scan based on variations of the ideas presented here. However, we believe this system reflects an honest, useful, and respectable approach to metrics and scansion. We think it is particularly effective for the beginning student of the subject and flexible enough to be useful to the advanced student.

Some terms used by those who write about meter are standard, like the names for feet, line lengths, and types of poems and stanzas. Other terms used here are less familiar. Those related to how we determine stress and names for "kinds of stress" are our own.

This book is not intended to be read straight through. Some concepts are explained more than once at different levels of complexity.

1 How to Read a Poem

Before we begin defining and analyzing meter and metrical effects, we would like to put metrical analysis and the process of reading poems into a clearer perspective. It is possible to read poems well without knowing very much about meter. If you are in the habit of reading closely—rereading to make sure you understand all the parts, looking up words, finding and considering **allusions**, being attentive to **tone**, and knowing how to read **irony**—then reading poems should be fairly easy for you. Yet most people are so intimidated by the thought of reading poems that they don't even know where to start. They don't know how rich and rewarding the reading of poetry can be. So we thought that if we could reduce the potential for confusion and angry denunciations by giving readers strategies for making poems more immediately comprehensible, then we ought to do that *before* we begin discussing the niceties of poetic meter.

When we began to put this book together, our primary concerns were to make the reading of poetry easier and to show how understanding meter increases our appreciation for poetry. We do not want to overemphasize the importance of metrical analysis, but we do want to show you how it is done and why. A study of meter not only deepens your poem-reading experiences, it can also show you why advertising jingles get stuck in our heads, why certain lines from songs are memorable, why certain passages in prose are poetic, and why nursery rhymes and jump-rope songs are so easy to remember.

Poetry should be read like any other writing—with the desire to understand what the writer has to say about a particular topic. Many beginning readers of poetry are discouraged by what they perceive as "elevated" or difficult language. They are used to reading journalism, business reports, how-to books, comics, or magazine articles. So when they encounter a piece of writing that they must reread two or three times to understand, they get annoyed and impatient. They may even get angry at what seems an assault on their intelligence. They immediately criticize poetry as overly sophisticated, arcane, or unrelated to their lives. Yet poetry is absolutely about how well we lead our lives; it challenges our assumptions, asks us to question or reaffirm what we do and how we feel. It is constantly in the business of regarding the human and natural world with a curious, suspicious eye.

It is true that some poetry can be difficult and challenges us even after a number of serious readings. Sometimes the poet nods, sometimes we do. But the essential point is that we lead difficult, complicated lives; our world is changing rapidly and old values need examination and perhaps modification to accommodate these changes. Complicated poems often merely reflect the complexity of the issues one needs to address simultaneously in our world, where religious, ethnic, social, economic, and philosophical assurances often compete or conflict. The important thing is not to feel intimidated by such poems, but to try to use all your critical and interpretive strategies for coming to terms with them.

There are several general strategies for getting closer to poems and some local, specific ones as well. Perhaps the most inclusive strategy is understanding the poems' explicit and implicit narrative signals. Even **lyric** poems often have a **narrative** context—a time, a place, a situation. We first need to find out what happens and to whom, what are the motives and motivations, what are the competing perspectives. We can also read for depictions of emotions or lyrical expressiveness. This is usually an analysis or illustration of what someone feels as a consequence of some action or experience. We can read for surprising language and the interplay of sounds. Is there a "sweet articulation" of sounds, fresh **metaphors**, interesting and engaging sentences, and well-turned phrases?

We may also read for voice: the evidence of a sympathetic and empathetic consciousness, a fellow traveler in a world we recognize as our own. Or if your taste is not for empathy and you would rather be in the company of an angry nihilist whose voyage through the world is marked by loud, satirical, swashbuckling bravado, then there are those voices to listen to as well. Different voices match particular moods and experiences, and we find ourselves attracted to different writers at different stages of our lives.

Good poetry is wonderful reading because it rewards us on almost all of these levels simultaneously. When we are in the realm of a good poem, we feel like rats with paws on the pleasure-levers. We read a line or two and stop to let the electric tingles hum and buzz. Yet it is only through practice that this pleasure is repeatedly available to us. The more we read, the easier it gets. It is like learning how to appreciate good wine or food or music. This multiplicity of rewards, by the way, should convince you that just knowing what a poem "means" is a meager way to relate to it. It's the equivalent of taking vitamins or starch and protein supplements rather than eating the foods you love. When you have savored the flavors of a poem and tried to understand their components, you'll be able to appreciate the nuances much more completely and with more fulfillment.

In "The Figure a Poem Makes" Robert Frost wrote that poetry was a "momentary stay against confusion." He was describing the process of writing poems and compared it to the progress of love: "it begins in delight, it inclines to the impulse, it assumes direction with the first line laid down, it runs a course of lucky events, and ends in a clarification of life—not necessarily a great clarification, such as sects and cults are founded on, but in a momentary stay against confusion" (1995, 777). By following the poem from start to finish, we have as a result a kind of snapshot, a frozen frame, of our ongoing experience. If we look carefully at this snapshot, we can see much of the chaos that is its background. We can zero in on the action and thus observe technique, method, or the underpinning mechanisms at work. Although a poem may reveal a principle important to us, an aspect of an idea we had forgotten, we should always be aware of the whole process—how this slice of life fits back into the pie.

Although this is a book about appreciating the metrical aspects of poems, we don't want to give you the impression that meter or any of the other formal qualities of poetry associated with it should be your primary interest while reading a poem. What the poem is about and how it explores that material is more important than the technical means it uses. Yet by focusing on those means, we can perhaps get closer to finding out why we felt what we felt. That process can deepen our reading, enhance it, complicate it. We should have gotten very close to what the subject matter of a poem is before we figure out how it dealt with that subject matter. Occasionally, a metrical analysis will reveal tones and nuances unavailable at the first or second reading; for example, it may reveal places where the poet was being ironic when we thought he or she was serious.

Here is a brief list of things to do and questions to answer before going on to a metrical analysis. They address what the poem is about before we look at how it achieves that meaning.

1. Look up words you don't know or have suspicions the poet is using in a peculiar way. Often fairly common words have more than one meaning. For example, the common definition of "depend" is to "rely on for support or aid." Yet the last definition in the *American Heritage Dictionary* is "to hang down," so we could say that an apple depended from its branch.

2. Look carefully at the pronouns. Who is speaking? To whom?

Does the poet seem to be in sympathy with the **speaker**? Is he or she critical of the person spoken to? Which details seem to support your reading? Which may contradict it? Are there any vague pronouns—*it, this, what*—that seem to have no antecedents or can apply to more than one thing? Does this seem purposeful or merely confusing? Why? What is the situation—the place or setting, the characteristics of the conversation?

3. Which words seem to mean more than one thing? What language seems to be **figurative** and what seems to be **literal**? What are the **metaphors** or **similes**? Any **personifications**? Which meaning or meanings, then, does the poet seem to want to draw on? Why?

4. What are the emotional issues at stake? Does the speaker seem to be angry at the person he or she addresses? Is there resentment, love, curiosity, embarrassment, admiration? What seems to convey this emotional attitude? Whom should the reader side with and why?

5. What are the intellectual issues at stake? What ideas seem to be of primary interest to the writer? How we regard nature in a value-less universe? How we may live deeply despite our self-consciousness, which may undermine positive action? How we may lead spiritual lives given contemporary constraints? How mind and body articulate their demands? For example, if the poem seems to be about unrequited love, what evidence does the speaker give to illustrate the lover's lack of attention or care? Why should we believe the speaker? Has he or she earned our respect? How? Where?

6. What seems to be the prevailing **tone**? Which words seem to convey that tone most strongly?

These are just a few things to do before attempting any metrical analysis. **Scansion** can help us clear up some of these questions, but it is only one of a number of strategies for deepening our understanding of any particular poem.

We will demonstrate this strategy by looking at a poem by Thomas Hardy.

Moments of Vision

That mirror
Which makes of men a transparency,
Who holds that mirror
And bids us such a breast-bare spectacle see
Of you and me?
That mirror
Whose magic penetrates like a dart,

Who lifts that mirror
And throws our mind back on us, and our heart,
 Until we start?
 That mirror
 Works well in these night hours of ache;
 Why in that mirror
Are tincts we never see ourselves once take
 When the world is awake?
 That mirror
 Can test each mortal when unaware;
 Yea, that strange mirror
May catch his last thoughts, whole life foul or fair,
 Glassing it—where?

1. The words that seem curious and might need some clarification are *transparency, spectacle, tincts,* and *start. Transparency* is the noun form of the more common adjective *transparent,* which means "capable of transmitting light so that objects or images can be seen as if there were no intervening materials" and "easily understood or detected" and "guileless or candid." *Spectacle* means "a public display" and "an object of interest or curiosity" or "an object or scene regrettably exposed to the public gaze" or "the sight of something"—it comes from a Latin word meaning "to look at." *Tincts* is an archaic word meaning "color or tint"; it is also a shortening of *tincture,* which means "a dyeing substance" and "a quality that colors, pervades, or distinguishes," and "a trace, a vestige." *Start* is a common word, but Hardy seems to be using an uncommon meaning of it. We know it means to begin or commence, but it also means to "move suddenly or involuntarily." It seems to have come from the word "startle": "to cause to make a quick involuntary movement" or "to alarm, frighten, or surprise."

2. In the fourth line, the poet refers to an "us," and in the fifth, to a "you and me." He seems to be speaking from the first person (*I*) directly to the reader (*you*). He assumes that the reader has had the same experiences with these moments of vision that he does. He wants his experience to relate to ours. The "who" in the third line of the second stanza doesn't seem to have a clear antecedent. In fact, there seems to be some slight confusion between the "whose" in the previous line, which clearly referred to "mirror," and this "who," which "lifts that mirror." The best guess is that "who" refers to anyone who lifts the mirror, who is willing to be self-reflective at night. The speaker seems to be alone, talking to an indistinct general audience. He refers to "these

night hours," and he is in plain view of a mirror. Perhaps he is in his bedroom (a likely place for a mirror), sleepless, and letting his mind wander.

3. The metaphors are the "mirror," "transparency," "spectacle," "magic," "tincts," "dart," and "night." The mirror seems to be both a literal mirror and figuratively any "reflection," any "moment of vision" that allows us a deep look into ourselves. "Transparency" is a mirror word and suggests that the image of ourselves is candid, guileless, and full of light. Our inmost selves are spotlighted until we see the inner man or woman. "Spectacle" suggests something seen as well as an object regrettably exposed. If we make a spectacle of ourselves, we become curious objects to the others around us. In this poem, the longer we look at ourselves, the more like curious objects we become. "Magic" is an emotional word here, suggesting how the speaker feels about being his own spectacle. This sudden self-exposure seems magical, unreal. "Tincts" is a strange word but also very apt. At this strange night hour, we see distinguishing characteristics, pervading qualities, which may not be very attractive. We see traces of our old selves, we see vestiges of animal behavior, we see human nature (especially ours!) suddenly revealed. This revelation penetrates like a "dart," a poisoned arrow, perhaps some sharp, painful awareness. "Night" is both literal and figurative. The poem takes place in the dark, but this setting suggests that we can only have such a moment of vision or awareness when all daytime distractions are gone. We look squarely into the unknown, into uncertainty, perhaps into our own mortality. What we see causes an involuntary reaction, a "start." This surprise "starts" us thinking even more deeply, so Hardy seems to be using the word both ways.

4. The emotional issues are centered in words like "dart" and "throws" and "ache." The dart implies that there is a sudden painful and emotional awakening. The "throws" implies that the emotional effect is involuntary and knocks us around a bit. The "ache" is a clear emotional statement: the speaker feels that this stab of self-awareness is a consequence of a number of "night hours" spent pondering one's state. Even a word like "Yea" has a bit of feeble self-consolation in it; it is as if he has to talk himself into making some broader general statement here.

5. The intellectual issues at stake concern those aspects of human nature that are unsavory: what do we do with painful moments of vision when we see ourselves revealed and don't particularly like what

we see? Poets and philosophers have been trying to solve this problem for thousands of years. Are our bad qualities devil-sponsored? Are they a product of having eaten from the tree of knowledge? Were our bodies temporarily inhabited by a vengeful god? Was the bad behavior merely an emanation, a black bubble, from our subconscious? These questions have been pondered for years with a variety of solutions. Hardy addresses this debate to give us another way to think about the issues involved. The steady repetition of the word "mirrors" suggests that Hardy is most persistently criticizing the "glassing" we normally do—that which helps us put on a mask so that we make ourselves look better. The depth of our delusions is suddenly realized when we have one of these profound moments, one of these night visions, where we see ourselves plainly.

6. The prevailing tone seems to be a suppressed bitterness. The speaker doesn't like what he sees in himself late at night, but he doesn't whine and moan about it. He just records the experience, the observation, and wonders "where" this kind of self-reflection can lead, especially if we judge our lives as being "foul." It isn't so bad if we think all has been "fair," but words like "ache" and "thrown" suggest he might be inclined toward the "foul."

If we did a metrical analysis of this poem, we would discover that the meter supports the "ache," the despairing qualities, but it is more important to do this kind of reading and analysis before scanning because then we know the parameters of the debate, what the issues are.

2 An Introduction to Meter

Poetic **meter** is based on recurring units of measurement. There are four measuring systems used by poets. (1) **Quantitative verse** depends upon a consistent interplay of long and short syllables; classical meters are quantitative. (2) **Accentual verse** depends upon a consistent number of **accents** or stresses, regardless of how many unstressed syllables are around them; Old English meters are accentual. (3) **Syllabic verse** depends on a consistent number of syllables in each **line**, regardless of where the stresses happen to fall; Japanese verse often uses this meter. (4) **Accentual-syllabic verse** depends upon a consistent interplay of stressed and unstressed syllables; meter in English is primarily accentual-syllabic.

Syllables are the basic sound units in words that govern how we pronounce them. In most dictionaries, the divisions between syllables are illustrated with dots (*po•et•ry*), and the pronunciation key in parentheses after the word tells where the accents or stresses are (*pō´•ĭ•trē*). The primary and secondary stresses are given for longer words. For example, *pho•to•syn•the•sis* has these accent marks (fo´•to•sin´•the•sis´).

Accentual-syllabic meter in English is the deliberate arrangement of syllables and their stresses to achieve a particular sound effect. That is the meter we will consider in this book.

Stress refers to the way we pronounce our words—which syllables in a word are pronounced more emphatically than others around them, which syllables in a line are stronger than the ones around them. For example, if we look up a word like *forgotten* in the dictionary, we are told that it is pronounced like this: (for•got´•ten). The dominant syllable is "-got"; it is stressed. If we take a word like *haberdasher*, we will notice how the first syllables are marked: (hab-) stressed, (-ber) unstressed, (-dash) stressed, (-er) unstressed. The symbol we use to mark a strong stress is `. An unstressed syllable is marked with a ˘. Poets use patterns of accented and unaccented syllables to create a particular meter or to achieve a particular effect. If you look carefully at the meter of a common children's rhyme, you will see how this works:

<pre>
    `   ˘   `   ˘   `   ˘   `
Jack and Jill went up the hill
</pre>

˘   `   ˘   `   ˘   `   ˘

To fetch a pail of water.

`   ˘   `   ˘   `   ˘   `

Jack fell down and broke his crown

˘   `   ˘   `   ˘   `   ˘

And Jill came tumbling after.

In the first line, the most obvious stressed syllables are "Jack," "Jill," and "hill." The only question may be about "went" versus "up." Yet we have created such a precedent with the first three syllables that expectation forces us to keep the rhythm going. If we reversed the position of "went" and "up"—so the line read, "Jack and Jill up went the hill"—then the stress would fall on "went." The second line is easy because the first two stresses are on large-sounding one-syllable words—"fetch," "pail"—and the last stress on "wa-" falls predictably into place. The "fell" in the third line is a bit troublesome, but it is enclosed by stronger syllables and the singsong rhythm of the earlier lines represses it. Also, "fell down" is what linguists call a phrasal verb. This means that "down" is acting as part of the verb, as a *particle* and not a preposition. Often phrasal verbs take on idiomatic meaning beyond what the verb and preposition might mean separately. For example, "passed out" (as in a drunken coma), "called off" (as in canceling), and "took off" (as in a speedy exit) are phrasal verbs with specialized meanings, so the particles are important and can take a stress. In the line "Jack went up the hill," the "went up" is not a phrasal verb because "up the hill" is a prepositional phrase, but in the sentence "I went up yesterday," the "went up" is phrasal. In a book on teaching English as a second language called *The Grammar Book*, the authors note that "another formal difference between a verb + preposition and a phrasal verb is that a particle may receive stress, whereas a preposition usually doesn't" (Celce-Murcia and Larsen-Freeman 1999, 431). However, the metrical environment of poems has components and expectations that are absent in normal speech, so prepositions often get **metrical stresses** rather than rhetorical ones. Particles, though, can get a **rhetorical stress** (these terms are explained fully on pages 16–17).

In English, we group accented and unaccented syllables into units called **feet**. The following quick explanation will be expanded later; don't worry if this version is not entirely clear. English poets use only seven kinds of metrical feet. The names of these feet and the patterns of accented and unaccented syllables they represent are as follows: **iamb**

(˘˘), **trochee** (˘˘), **anapest** (˘˘˘), **dactyl** (˘˘˘), **spondee** (˘˘), **pyrrhic** (˘˘), and **monosyllabic foot** (˘). The foot is the basic unit of measurement in a line. When we **scan** a line, we look for combinations of accented and unaccented syllables and group them into these feet. Note that the trochee is a reversed iamb, and that a dactyl is a reversed anapest. We often call the substitution of one for the other a **reversed foot**.

The two odd feet here are the monosyllabic foot and the pyrrhic. The monosyllabic foot has only one syllable, but it is understood that it is missing an unstressed syllable, much as in a contraction. When we see "I'm," we know an "a" is missing. The monosyllabic foot frequently occurs at the beginning or end of a line. In trochaic meters, for example, it is common to find a monosyllabic foot at the end because the poet wants the line to finish strongly. Consider William Blake's "The Tyger": "Tyger, tyger burning bright, / In the forests of the night." This is in trochaic **tetrameter** (lines of four trochees) and in place of the last trochee there is a single stress, a monosyllabic foot. Conversely, an iambic line can begin with a stress—either a monosyllabic foot or a spondee. The poet occasionally wants to begin a line strongly to vary the tempo.

The most problematic foot is the pyrrhic. There has been much critical debate about this foot. Some theorists maintain that it doesn't exist, and others tend to see it frequently. One of the most basic definitions of meter is "regularly recurring stress," and clearly a pyrrhic foot has no stress. Essentially, we find metrical stresses where many of the other critics find pyrrhics. We believe the pyrrhic is rare in English **prosody** and is most common in what we call a **super-iamb**: a pyrrhic followed by a spondee (˘˘|˘˘). Here, it is as if two iambs underwent some atomic fusion and recombined in a new way. The super-iamb occurs most often at the beginning or end of the line but is occasionally found in the middle. For a more complete discussion of the pyrrhic, see Chapter 11, "Some Fine Points." W. B. Yeats is particularly fond of super-iambs, and they have been used effectively by William Wordsworth, John Keats, and Robert Frost. There are several examples in Yeats's "Adam's Curse," found on pages 63–66.

The seven metrical feet are like metrical primary colors from which almost any metrical effect can be made. The terms we use for the feet are Latinized versions of Greek words, though Greek meter is very different from that used in English. In English, a foot is the combination of syllables that make up the basic sound units for measuring a line of verse. **Verse** comes from the Latin word "versus" meaning "a turning of the plow." A **line** is a unit, after which the reader "re-turns" to start a new line.

We call the analysis of metrical effects **prosody**, and the marking of unaccented and accented syllables **scansion**. Greek meter was based on the duration of a syllable, and English meter is based on stress, so some of the poetic terms and assumptions that govern Greek prosody do not translate clearly into the ways we use them. A few English poets have tried to write in strict Greek meters, but when they have, the resulting poems have borne little relation to the auditory effects in Greek.

In accentual-syllabic verse, the measurement is based on the regular recurrence of stress. You must learn to recognize the seven basic feet mentioned above so that you can divide a line into these feet. When we name a line's meter, we name the predominant foot (iamb, trochee, etc.) and then name the number of such units to a line. Thus, an iambic **pentameter** line is one that consists of five feet, the majority of which are iambs. If you had three iambs to the line, then you would have iambic **trimeter**. If you had three trochees, it would still be trimeter, but now it would be called trochaic trimeter. If you had four feet, then it would be called **tetrameter**. The terms designating the number of units per line are derived from Greek and Latin numerical prefixes.

The number of feet in each line of poetry determines how we describe it. A poem whose lines have only one foot is in **monometer**; a line with two feet is called **dimeter**; three feet is called **trimeter**; four, **tetrameter**; five, **pentameter**; six, **hexameter**; seven, **heptameter**; and eight, **octameter**. Pentameter is the most common and popular of all poetic meters in English, followed by tetrameter and trimeter. There are also poems whose **stanzas** have varied line lengths. For example, a poem could have five-line stanzas, but the first line might be in pentameter, the second in tetrameter, the third in dimeter, the fourth in tetrameter, and the fifth in pentameter. Thomas Hardy was fond of creating stanzas with line lengths in odd patterns, and "Moments of Vision" is a good example; its stanzaic pattern is 1-4-2-5-2 (a monometer line, followed by tetrameter, dimeter, pentameter, and dimeter). We will be discussing these patterns more completely in Chapter 6.

One of the reasons the pentameter line is popular is that it corresponds to what we can say in a single breath. Longer lines tend to become ungainly. In his "Essay On Criticism" Alexander Pope complains about the eighteenth-century habit of ending pentameter poems with an **alexandrine** (a line with six feet, i.e., in hexameter): "A needless Alexandrine ends the song / That like a wounded snake, drags its slow length along." Pope's lines perfectly illustrate his complaint: the first line is pentameter and moves swiftly, the second is hexameter and the spondees (snake/drags and slow/length) slow it down to the speed of a crippled snake. This slowness, however, is more a function of the spondees in the line than of the extra foot. Even a line of trimeter can seem slow if it has two spondees in it.

Later in the same poem, Pope describes the way sounds should echo the sense a poet wishes to convey:

> 'Tis not enough no harshness gives offence,
> The sound must seem an echo to the sense.
> Soft is the strain when Zephyr gently blows,
> And the smooth stream in smoother numbers flows;
> But when loud surges lash the sounding shore
> The hoarse, rough verse should like the torrent roar.
> When Ajax strives, some rock's vast weight to throw,
> The line too labours, and the words move slow.

In an era when metrical poetry was the only kind being written, pedantic critics would measure a poet's worth by how consistent and flawless his or her meter was. This criterion was common up until the first half of the twentieth century. "Harshness" or a rough meter—meter that had many deviations from the norm, that used many **substitutions**—would offend these sticklers for regularity, and Pope is arguing that one's appreciation of meter should be more complex than mere consistency. The "sound must seem an echo to the sense," he says, and illustrates what he means in the next few lines. In Greek mythology, Zephyrus was the god personifying the gentle west wind, so if he were to enter one's poem, one would need a gentle meter; this is why Pope, in the third line, uses a trochee followed by an iamb (the effect of an anapest) and regular iambs thereafter—resulting in a soft, gentle rhythm. In the fourth line, he illustrates the harshness of waves crashing on the shore metrically, with spondees; he starts the line with an iamb, which he follows with a spondee:

$$\breve{} \quad \grave{} \mid \grave{} \quad \grave{} \mid \breve{} \quad \grave{} \mid \breve{} \quad \grave{} \mid \breve{} \quad \grave{}$$

but when loud surges lash the sounding shore

The effect is three stresses in a row, and "lash" is a strong, harsh syllable as well. Of course, the **alliteration** of the "l," "s," and "sh" sounds, and the **assonance** of the "ou" sounds, also reinforce Pope's metrical choices. There are also three stresses in the subsequent line: the initial iamb is followed by a spondee and the syllables are large and mouth-filling, which makes the line discordant, makes it "roar." Not only should the physical, natural world be described with this kind of auditory effect, but powerful human action as well. Ajax is a strong warrior in Homer's *Iliad;* when he performs some superhuman feat, the meter should match the action—the "sound" of the passage should echo the "sense" Homer wished to convey to the reader.

Besides regarding the metrical pattern in a poem to determine its form, we also look at its **rhyme scheme**. The sequencing of rhymed syllables at the ends of lines is plotted so that we can see what pattern the poet has chosen. Certain patterns are associated with the poets who frequently used them. For example, **terza rima** is written in three-line stanzas whose first and third lines rhyme, while the second line's end word becomes the first and third **rhyme** of the next stanza. This pattern is associated with Dante Alighieri's *Divine Comedy* and is also employed by Percy Bysshe Shelley in his "Ode to the West Wind":

> O wild West Wind, thou breath of Autumn's being,
> Thou, from whose unseen presence the leaves dead
> Are driven, like ghosts from an enchanter fleeing,
>
> Yellow, and black, and pale, and hectic red,
> Pestilence-stricken multitudes: O thou,
> Who chariotest to their dark wintry bed . . .

We will discuss **stanza** forms later, and there is a glossary of them in the back of this book, but notice how we plot the rhyme scheme of the following poem, "Resolve," by Mark Halperin:

The day comes when the bird *feeder*	a
stands empty and the fatted junco *settles*	b
into feathers on the branch, when no dog, *either*	a
young or old, will bark, and *kettles*	b
hold their breath. The morning *arrives*	c
when there's no light, when the blankets are *lead*	d
and vampires, call them work or the mundane in our *lives,*	c
guard the ways out, when I've *considered*	d
the clock on my shelf or in my gut, *flinched*	e
one more time, then marked *Finished*	e
to the claims of infant and parent. Let the *sky*	f
close, I think, were I my own, were *I* . . .	f
So, like the poor, I atone for the *sins*	g
I couldn't commit, and my resolve, of itself, *softens.*	g

This poem starts out like a Shakespearean **sonnet** with an alternating (*ababcdcd* . . .) pattern of rhyme, but it switches in the tenth line to **couplets**. The meter is also loose and variable; it seems to fluctuate between a four- and a five-stress line. Note that the rhymes are not "full" or complete; they often depend on subtler sound connections, which is typical of the twentieth-century poem, in which poetic effects are more often disguised than made apparent. Because this poem is rhymed and has fourteen lines, we would call it a sonnet; because its rhyme scheme has such strong connections to the Shakespearean sonnet (even to the couplet at the end), yet takes off on its own, and its meter is so variable, we can easily identify it as a modern sonnet. It is best to plot the rhyme scheme of several stanzas so that you are sure of the pattern. Had we plotted only the first eight lines here, we would not have known that Halperin altered the typical pattern.

3 Scansion: A Practical Guide

Meters are like keys in music: they don't have particular effects. None are intrinsically sad, happy, or jolly. But just as minor keys are more conducive to sad songs, certain meters generally work out better in some contexts than in others. Metrical feet are made up of combinations of stressed and unstressed syllables. In marking them off, we may discover that the last syllable of one word and the first syllable of another make up a single foot. This may make little sense, but think of measure-lines in music: sometimes they appear in the middle of a word for vocal music. It causes no problems there, and foot boundaries in meter should cause no trouble in scansion.

Most people are neither tone-deaf nor do they have perfect pitch. We all have a good sense of relative pitch that can be developed. The same is true with our metrical sensitivity to poems. Most people do not have "tin ears." With practice we find ourselves more and more sensitive to the metrical component of poetry.

The purpose of studying metrics is to become aware of the regularity underlying metrical verse and the departures from that regularity. You can't enjoy syncopated rhythms unless you know what the basic pulse is; you don't enjoy variations on a tune unless you know what the basic tune is. All this is obvious in music and equally true of metrical poetry. To start with, you've got to determine the basic metrical pattern. Only then can you concern yourself with deviations from it.

In English, the accent occurs at the beginning or end of the foot (or both for spondees). The iamb and the anapest are seen as "rising" because they end with an accent; the trochee and dactyl are seen as "falling" because they end with an unaccented syllable.

There are only two basic arrangements of accents in English: alternating accents (i.e., every other syllable) or accents separated by two unaccented syllables. All feet are either **disyllabic** (iambic or trochaic), or **trisyllabic** (anapestic or dactylic). Therefore, if the start of a line is most often unaccented, the rhythm will probably be **rising**. If it is accented, the rhythm will probably be **falling**.

Determining meter is difficult at times because all accents don't have the same force. A word like "squinch" has to be accented, but a preposition like "to" might also be accented in the same line. Meter builds up a pattern of **expectation**. The previously quoted lines of Blake demonstrate this clearly: "Tyger, tyger burning bright, / In the forests of the night." Notice how the "of" in the second line gets accented. In a metrical environment some of these shorter, softer syllables get a light stress. This maintains the metrical feel of the line. Our expectation of the pattern is not disturbed; it is merely downplayed to make the line more like speech. When a syllable can't take a stress, then expectations are denied and syncopation and other emphatic effects follow. Even differences in the degrees of stress cause lines to sound different; we will discuss that in more detail later.

While investigating the reasons certain syllables get stressed in a line and others don't, we determined that there are basically three ways of accounting for the occurrence of stress. We have used different terms merely to help determine whether a syllable is stressed. These ways all work together and can overlap, but we think this method for viewing stress will help clarify where and why stress occurs.

lexical stress: "Lexical" comes from the word *lexicon*, which means "dictionary" or "word stock." A lexical stress is the stress in a polysyllabic word as indicated by the dictionary. Polysyllabic words in English have a primary stress, which tells us how to pronounce them. They may also have secondary stresses; these can be looked up in the dictionary. Earlier we pointed out that "photosynthesis" has these accent marks (fo´•to•sin´•the•sis´). Remember that words with only one syllable will not be marked with an accent or stress in the dictionary. The dictionary only shows the accent in words with more than one syllable.

rhetorical stress: We chose the word "rhetorical" because it refers to the art of effective expression and the persuasive use of language. Rhetorical stresses are contextual; the meaning of the line will focus a little spotlight on a particular monosyllabic word when a sentence is pronounced as it would be in speech. Usually, the word that is conveying important information gets a rhetorical stress. For example, Keats's sonnet "On First Looking into Chapman's Homer" starts with these two lines: "Much have I traveled in the realms of gold, / And many goodly states and kingdoms seen." The accent on "much" is a rhetorical stress; Keats wants to emphasize how much he has traveled through book kingdoms so that his praise of Chapman's translations of Homer is given some context.

metrical stress: Metrical stress is a stress that is neither of the above; it occurs on a syllable that can bear a stress, never an indefinite or definite article (*a, the*), though often a preposition and occasionally on a conjunction (*and, but, yet, so*). Expectation drives this stress; if a strong meter is established and the reader runs into three or four weak syllables in a row, then the metrical pattern will assert itself, and one of those weak syllables will be stressed. This stress is light and you should not try to plot it until the other two kinds of stresses are determined. (For a special note on trisyllabic meters see Chapter 11, "Some Fine Points.")

Prescansion Exercise

Mark the syllables in the following words as being either stressed or unstressed; if these words were in a poem, we would be marking their lexical stresses (see page 81 for scansion).

1. ob-ser-va-tion
2. pan-the-on
3. par-tic-u-lar
4. de-bat-a-ble
5. diagonal
6. devotional
7. graduation
8. independent
9. liberty
10. moderate

Scan the following lines:

1. The sea is calm tonight (Matthew Arnold, "Dover Beach")
2. The tide is full, the moon lies fair (Arnold)
3. Its melancholy, long withdrawing roar (Arnold)
4. Come to the window, sweet is the night air (Arnold)
5. Much have I traveled in the realms of gold (John Keats)
6. And many goodly states and kingdoms seen (Keats)
7. Thy soul was like a star, and dwelt apart (William Wordsworth, "London, 1802")
8. Thou hadst a voice whose sound was like the sea (Wordsworth)
9. Pure as the naked heavens, majestic, free (Wordsworth)
10. Your door is shut against my tightened face (Claude McKay, "The White House")

11. We passed the School, where Children strove (Emily Dickinson, "Because I could not stop for Death")

12. We passed the fields of Gazing Grain (Dickinson)

13. I lean and loaf at my ease observing a spear of summer grass (Walt Whitman, "Song of Myself")

14. I love thee with the passion put to use (Elizabeth Barrett Browning, "Sonnets from the Portuguese 43")

15. In my old griefs, and with my childhood's faith. (Browning)

Steps for Determining Meter in a Poem

1. Read the poem (or a representative group of lines) aloud several times. Listen to how the language rolls off your tongue. When you work with a poem, always use several lines so that some local oddness does not overly influence your scansion.

2. Mark off all the syllables in each line; if you are confused about syllable divisions, look the word up in the dictionary.

3. Find the obvious lexical stresses in each line. This means that you must work with the polysyllabic words first. Pronounce them conscientiously and listen for the primary stress. You should hear it clearly. If the word is long, listen for the secondary stress, or look the word up in a dictionary. Mark all primary and secondary stresses. A dictionary is useful because a word like "impulse" seems to have a long second syllable, but if you listen closely, you discover that the accent is on the first syllable—a dictionary will help you hear when your mind gets a little crowded with the anxiety of having to hear "correctly."

4. Determine and mark the rhetorical stresses. To do this, read the line as if it were prose. What do you accent? You will only have monosyllabic words to consider, since step three took care of the polysyllabic words. Generally, the principal components of the sentence pick up stresses—verbs, objects, and some adverbs and adjectives that mark shifts in the meaning of the line. Pronouns are flexible and will often take metrical stresses, but occasionally they will take rhetorical stresses if the meaning seems to pivot on them.

5. Now look for a pattern of stresses. Do stresses occur on every other syllable, every third syllable? If you have marked enough lines and the poem is metered traditionally, one of these two patterns should show up.

6. Mark all remaining syllables unaccented. This is the time to determine the metrical stresses. Are there any syllables that could be lightly

stressed that would fit the pattern? Good places to look are long un-stressed sequences of syllables. Don't distort accent, but remember that a syllable in a metrical environment may be stressed when it wouldn't be in a **free-verse** poem.

7. Divide the line into feet. This division marker is called a **vir-gule (I)**. After you have decided which foot predominates (generally iambs or trochees), you should try to make your foot divisions fit your pattern. For example, the line

　　　` ˘ ` ˘ ` ˘ ` ˘ ` ˘

Sounding out how high a space, or shallow

could be read as trochaic pentameter, but most of the lines in the poem are iambic pentameter. If we mark the initial foot as monosyllabic, then we have preserved four iambs (the unaccented syllable at the end doesn't count).

　　　` |˘ ` | ˘ ` | ˘ ` | ˘ ` | ˘

Sounding out how high a space, or shallow.

Incidentally, to indicate which foot in a line you are talking about, number from the beginning of the line. A poem in trimeter has a first, a second, and a third foot. The third would be the last foot in the trimeter line.

8. Read the poem or passage out loud again. Does your analysis agree with what you hear? It should. Remember that a metrical poem follows a regular pattern more often than not. When there are several possible ways of scanning a line, choose the one that has fewer variations.

9. Don't be overly ingenious. Most poets who write in meter strive for regularity. The pattern is the norm, and you are looking for the norm. **Variations** are used for emphasis and variety.

Application of These Scansion Steps

We would now like to illustrate how we can apply these steps to a poem; we've chosen Theodore Roethke's "My Papa's Waltz."

1. The whiskey on your breath
2. Could make a small boy dizzy;
3. But I held on like death:
4. Such waltzing was not easy.

5. We romped until the pans
6. Slid from the kitchen shelf;
7. My mother's countenance
8. Could not unfrown itself.

9. The hand that held my wrist
10. Was battered on one knuckle;
11. At every step you missed
12. My right ear scraped a buckle.

13. You beat time on my head
14. With a palm caked hard by dirt,
15. Then waltzed me off to bed
16. Still clinging to your shirt.

Step 1: Lexical Stress

We start by breaking the lines into syllables. "Whiskey" has two syllables; "breath," for all its length, is one. "Waltzing" and "dizzy" are two syllables, as is "easy." In the next stanza "kitchen," "mother's," "unfrown," and "itself" are two syllables, and "countenance" is three—coun + ten + ance. "Battered" and "every" are also two; so are "knuckle" and "buck-le." The "-le" sounds are just on the edge of being syllables, but since "knuck" and "buck" rhyme, we hear the final part as a separate syllable even if the vowel is only weakly there. In the last stanza only "clinging" has two syllables. The rest are one-syllable words.

Usually in a two-syllable word, the root gets the accent. So "waltz-," "diz-," "bat-" and "cling-" are all accented. In "itself," the accent is on the second syllable, but notice that this is a compound word. "Countenance" has its principal accent on the first syllable.

Step 2: Rhetorical Stress

Now we're ready to look for the rhetorical stresses. These tend to occur on monosyllabic words that carry most of the meaning. Often the pronoun that is the subject of a sentence is not stressed. We don't expect articles like "the" or "a" to be accented. And as for prepositions, we'll be returning to them, but, here, it's enough to remark that they generally are not good candidates for rhetorical stresses either.

So in the first line we accent "breath." In the second line, the verb "make" and probably both "small" and "boy" are stressed. In the third line we accent "I" because it's emphatic—it's preceded by a "but" and thus presents a contrast that is significant. The subject pronoun is often unaccented, but this contrast shifts the importance and emphasizes the "I." "Held," together with "on," functions as a phrasal verb (see earlier discussion of "Jack and Jill"). He didn't just "hold," he "held on," so it is possible to scan this as a spondee or as an iamb. "Death" is also accented because the word indicates how he "held on" and also rhymes with "breath." In the final line there are a number of possibilities. If you find "such" to be important because it particularizes the kind of waltzing the poet is referring to, then you'll accent it. "Was" is the verb, albeit a very weak one, and thus probably gets an accent. You might argue that "not" is also accented since it changes the meaning of "was" to "wasn't," but we don't hear it.

1. The whiskey on your breath

2. Could make a small boy dizzy;

3. But I held on like death:

4. Such waltzing was not easy.

In the next stanza, the first line "romped" receives an accent as the principal verb, but not "we," as is often the case with pronouns that are subjects. "Pans" is also accented. In the next line "slid," the verb, and "shelf," the object of the preposition, receive accents. In the third and fourth lines of the stanza, the possessive pronoun isn't accented, but "not" is.

5. We romped until the pans

6. Slid from the kitchen shelf;

7. My mother's countenance

8. Could not unfrown itself.

In the first line of the next stanza "hand," "held," and "wrist" are accented. In the third line "step" and "missed" are accented; in the fourth line "right," "ear," and "scraped" are accented as well.

⠀˘⠀⠀⠀`⠀⠀˘⠀⠀`⠀⠀⠀˘⠀`
9. The hand that held my wrist

⠀⠀˘⠀⠀`⠀⠀˘⠀⠀`⠀˘⠀⠀⠀`⠀˘
10. Was battered on one knuckle;

⠀⠀˘⠀⠀`⠀⠀˘⠀⠀⠀`⠀⠀˘⠀`⠀˘
11. At every step you missed

⠀˘⠀⠀`⠀⠀`⠀⠀⠀`⠀˘⠀`⠀⠀˘
12. My right ear scraped a buckle.

In the final stanza, we again pass up the "you," but do accent "beat time" and "head." In the next line "palm," "caked hard," and "dirt" are accented. The line that follows has accents on "waltzed" and "off" and "bed." In the final line "shirt" is accented.

⠀⠀˘⠀`⠀⠀⠀`⠀˘⠀⠀˘⠀⠀`
13. You beat time on my head

⠀⠀˘⠀⠀˘⠀`⠀⠀⠀`⠀⠀⠀`⠀˘⠀`
14. With a palm caked hard by dirt,

⠀⠀˘⠀⠀⠀`⠀⠀˘⠀˘⠀`
15. Then waltzed me off to bed

⠀⠀˘⠀⠀⠀`⠀˘⠀⠀˘⠀⠀`
16. Still clinging to your shirt.

We haven't mentioned stresses on the polysyllabic words, because we treated them earlier, under lexical stress. Now, after having considered these first two types of stress, can we see a pattern of either alternating accents or accents every three syllables? We want to have some idea of the pattern before we look for the final type of stress, metrical stress. In fact, some people might have argued for a few more accents, but the ones they probably would have chosen are the metrical stresses or accents that come from our expectation of the pattern. It's worth remembering that metrical accents are weaker than the ones we've marked so far. They occur on prepositions and syllables in polysyllabic words that are not adjacent to the principal stresses. We should find these weaker accents in what appear to be long, unaccented stretches. To find them we need to mark every syllable we haven't given a stress to with a tentative unstressed mark.

Step 3: Metrical Stress

It's hard to see a definite pattern here. Stretches in the poem where a number of accents are bunched together are confusing; they make the alternating pattern hard to find. By looking at lines 4, 5, 7, 8, 9, 11, and 15, however, we see a clear pattern of three iambs in a row, or iambic trimeter. With that in mind, let's take care of a few problems. If the poem is in iambic trimeter, we can disregard unaccented syllables at the ends of the lines (as in lines 2, 4, 10, and 12). We just say that the poem has some **falling rhymes** and dismiss the extra syllables. Usually, a poem in iambs will have spondees as variations, so we can look for those. Spondees provide accents where we expect them, but thicken the meter by turning what would be the unaccented syllable in an iamb into another accent. Spondees merely flavor the metrical taste of the line. Lines 2, 3, 12, 13, and 14 have spondees that seem to simply replace iambs that would have been in those positions. Lines 4 and 16 are still something of a problem.

With this in mind, let's go back to the first stanza:

1. The whiskey on your breath

2. Could make a small boy dizzy

3. But I held on like death:

4. Such waltzing was not easy

If the poem is in iambic trimeter, then the first line is missing an accent. Certainly the "-ey" in "whiskey" can't be accented since it's right next to the principal accent in the two-syllable word. "Your" could be accented if the poet wanted to emphasize possession here, but that's not the point. When we put a light metrical accent on "on," the rhythm that results seems quite natural. The next line needs no metrical accents. It's iamb, iamb, spondee (remember, we decided to forget about the extra syllable at the end because of the rhyme). In the third line, we have iamb, spondee, iamb. And in the final line of the stanza, we have an iamb (or a spondee if you accented "such"), an iamb, and an iamb, but "was not" could also be pronounced as a spondee. Even with the variations, the stanza sounds regular and smooth. When we write it out, we see that there are accents on every other syllable, and the extra stresses don't really change the pattern of expectation. All we might want to note is that there are a lot of spondees.

In the second stanza, there is more regularity.

˘　　ˋ　　˘　ˋ　˘　ˋ

We romped until the pans

ˋ　　˘　˘　ˋ　˘　ˋ

Slid from the kitchen shelf;

˘　　ˋ　˘　　ˋ　˘　ˋ

My mother's countenance

˘　　ˋ　˘　ˋ　˘　ˋ

Could not unfrown itself.

The first line is quite regular. The second line, though, has a substitution in its first foot—instead of an iamb (˘ˋ), there is a trochee (ˋ˘). When you expect a pattern and get the opposite, the disjunction produces emphasis. The word "slid" stands out and emphasizes the action of the pans. The third line appears to have a metrical accent on the last syllable of "coun-ten-ance." It's separated from the heavily accented first syllable and has a metrical stress because of expectation—not because it is a strong syllable. The fourth line is consistent with our pattern.

The third stanza is fairly regular as well:

˘　　ˋ　˘　ˋ　˘　ˋ

The hand that held my wrist

˘　　ˋ　˘　˘　ˋ　˘

Was battered on one knuckle;

˘　ˋ　˘　ˋ　˘　　ˋ

At every step you missed

˘　　ˋ　ˋ　ˋ　˘　ˋ　˘

My right ear scraped a buckle.

The only metrical accent is in the second line. There are three unaccented syllables in a row— "-ered," "on," one." In English, it is rare to have three unaccented syllables in a row because the middle one tends to rise to the accent. The iambic trimeter pattern suggests that "on" is accented, so we will put a metrical accent there. The last line has an iamb, a spondee, and an iamb in it.

In the fourth stanza, there are a number of variations.

˘   `   `   `   ˘   ˘   `
You beat time on my head

˘   ˘   `      `   `   ˘   `
With a palm caked hard by dirt,

˘   `   `   ˘   ˘   `
Then waltzed me off to bed

˘   `   `   ˘   ˘   `
Still clinging to your shirt.

The first line has an iamb, a trochee, and an iamb. The second starts with an anapest, which is followed by a spondee, and then an iamb; so there are two substitutions in this short line. In the third line "me," "off," and "to" are a sequence of weak syllables. There is some rhetorical significance to the word "off" because we're moving toward the conclusion of the dance and the poem. The pattern suggests that "off" is accented, so we will put a metrical accent there. In the last line, the three unaccented syllables are "-ing," "to," and "your." The "your" is the strongest syllable, but the pattern overrides its strength, and a metrical stress is put on "to." Again, it is possible to hear the first foot of the last line as a spondee, and if we say it that way the metrical variation created by the spondee at the beginning of the line has been brought back into the expected pattern.

If we put in virgules to mark off the feet, and take a look at what we've got, we can see that the basic meter is indeed iambic trimeter.

˘   `  |  ˘   ` | ˘   `
1. The whiskey on your breath

˘   `  |  ˘   ` | `    ` | ˘
2. Could make a small boy dizzy;

˘ `|  `   `  |  ˘      `   or
˘ `|  ˘   ` | ˘   `
3. But I held on like death:

˘   `  |  ˘   ` | `|˘   or
`      ` | ˘   `  |  ˘   `|˘
4. Such waltzing was not easy.

˘   `   |  ˘  ` | ˘   `
5. We romped until the pans

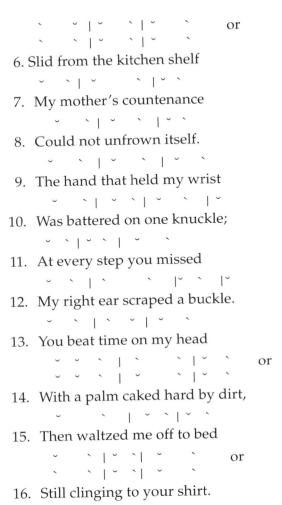

6. Slid from the kitchen shelf   or

7. My mother's countenance

8. Could not unfrown itself.

9. The hand that held my wrist

10. Was battered on one knuckle;

11. At every step you missed

12. My right ear scraped a buckle.

13. You beat time on my head   or

14. With a palm caked hard by dirt,

15. Then waltzed me off to bed   or

16. Still clinging to your shirt.

The "or" alternatives in lines 3, 4, 6, 14, and 16 are credible ways to pronounce these lines, and in fact each person might have some combination of these in his or her final scansion. Roethke's three-foot line makes sense because the poem is about a waltz. If you are familiar with music, you might make the association that three iambs to the line suggests waltz time, or 3/4 time, where three beats per measure is the distinctive characteristic. A poem called "My Papa's Waltz," which is about dancing, should mimic or establish a one-two-three, one-two-three feel. There are a number of spondees that give the poem a clotted or thickened sound, but the basic iambic pattern is apparent, and we get accents where we expect them.

More Scansion Examples

We would like to go over another poem in the same way to demonstrate this scanning method. Our assumption is that if you go through the poems slowly and methodically at first, then you can move more quickly later. This is the fourth of five sonnets in a series Joseph Powell has written about two sisters. Even without reading the others, the reader can figure out that there is a conflict between two people who see the world differently—the speaker is trying to understand her sister's mind. Let's take a look at this one metrically. The fact that this is a sonnet already colors our expectations about meter, but we can put that to one side for the time being.

Mirrors

1. From shade to darker shade, I walk her mind.
2. What help for those who grimly close us out
3. to prove some point or recompense unkind?
4. When we speak, I feel some mirror-light,
5. my ancient self, come back to haunt me now.
6. No word is word enough. No touch or look
7. suffices. My fingers lengthen like a shadow
8. and grip an empty sleeve, or stop a book.
9. His funeral gets larger every day:
10. her eyes have entered his blankest photographs.
11. She doesn't see mother, father, or me.
12. A broken doll, she looks at our tears, and laughs.
13. A ghost between us parts our common air—
14. immune to love, logic, our hardest prayers. (1993b, 37)

Step 1: Lexical Stress

If we divide the polysyllabic words into their syllables and establish the primary accent in each (we'll put it in caps) we come up with the following. In line 1, we find DARK-er. In line 2, there is GRIM-ly. Line 3 has RE-com-pense (secondary accent on "pense") and un-KIND. Line 4 has MIRR-or, and line 5 AN-cient. Line 6 has e-NOUGH, line seven suf-FIC-es, FIN-gers, LENG-then, and SHAD-ow. Line 8 has EMP-ty, and line 9 FUN-er-al, LARG-er, EV-er-y (but it is pronounced EV-ry). In line 10 we read: EN-tered, BLANK-est, and PHO-to-graphs. In the remaining lines, we have DOES-n't, MOTH-er, FA-ther, BROK-en, COM-mon, im-MUNE, LOG-ic, and HARD-est. Of course, there are some other possibilities. Isn't "prayers" pronounced like PRAY-airs by some?

However, most dictionaries treat it as a one-syllable word, and that is what we'll do.

Step 2: Rhetorical Stress

Now we will find the rhetorical accents. You should have some skill at this by now.

1. "Shade" is repeated, and each time it is accented. The verb "walk" is accented, and so is its object "mind." You should be getting used to the fact that the subject—in this case, "I"—is not always accented.

2. There are a number of ways to read this line. The simplest is to say "help," "those," "close," and "out" are all accented. The phrase "close out" is a verb phrase interrupted by "us," though some people might accent the "us" as well. The same people might also hear "what" being accented, as if it were acting like an adjective—the sort of help there is, which is no help.

3. Here, the obvious rhetorical accents are "prove" and "point."

4. The emphasis seems to be on the rarity of the speaking. So the accents fall on "when" and then the verb, "speak," followed by "feel," and "light."

5. This line is a little more ambiguous than the earlier ones. Certainly "self," "back," and "haunt" are accented. The action is embedded in "come back." The emphasis seems to be on "now" rather than "me," though both could be accented. Let's try the "now," and accent "come" as well.

6. Both references to "word" are accented, and "touch" and "look" are obviously accented.

7. This line seems to have only lexical accents. There is another accent, but it is one we will come back to later.

8. The accents here are easy to pick out: "grip," "sleeve," "stop," and "book."

9. There is only one rhetorical accent here, "day."

10. The line is very much like line 9. Its rhetorical accent is on "eyes."

11. Again the choices are easy: "see" and "me" are the only rhetorical accents in the line.

12. Here the words "doll," "looks," "tears," and "laughs" are all accented.

13. The main sentence words, "ghost," "parts," and "air"—subject, verb, and object—get the accents.

14. The final line accents "love" and "prayers."

Step 3: Metrical Stress

If we temporarily marked all the other syllables with unaccent marks, the scansion would look like this:

1. ˘ ˋ ˘ ˋ ˘ˋ ˘ ˋ ˘ˋ
2. ˘ ˋ ˘ ˋ ˘ˋ ˘ ˋ ˘ˋ
3. ˘ ˋ ˘ ˋ ˘ˋ ˘ ˘ ˘ˋ
4. ˋ ˘ ˋ ˘ˋ ˘ ˋ ˘ˋ
5. ˘ ˋ ˘ ˋ ˘ˋ ˘ ˋ ˘ˋ
6. ˘ ˋ˘ ˋ ˘ˋ ˘ ˋ ˘ ˋ
7. ˘ ˋ ˘˘ ˋ ˘ˋ ˘ ˘˘ ˋ˘
8. ˘ ˋ ˘ ˋ ˘ˋ ˘ ˋ ˘ ˋ
9. ˘ ˋ ˘ ˘ ˘ˋ ˘ ˋ ˘ ˋ
10. ˘ ˋ ˘ ˋ˘ ˘ˋ ˘ ˋ ˘ ˘
11. ˘ ˋ ˘ ˋ ˋ ˘ ˋ ˘ ˘ ˋ
12. ˘ ˋ ˘ ˋ ˘ˋ ˘ ˘ˋ ˘ ˋ
13. ˘ ˋ ˘ ˋ ˘ˋ ˘ ˋ ˘ˋ
14. ˘ ˋ ˘ ˋ ˋ˘ ˘ ˋ ˘ˋ

When we look at the result, there are a few places where accents are separated by two unaccented syllables, but the more common pattern is alternating accents, and all lines but the fourth start with an unaccented syllable. That strongly suggests an iambic pattern. The poem has fourteen lines with a rhyme scheme of *ababcdcdefef gg*. This is the scheme that Shakespeare used for his sonnets (see **sonnet** in the glossary). Sonnets are usually written in iambic pentameter. Our idea that this poem is iambic fits with what we know about sonnets in general.

Now, let's go through it line by line.

1. "From shade to darker shade, I walk her mind." This line is already completely scanned. It is iambic pentameter. We need only divide it into feet to see that: ˘ˋ | ˘ˋ | ˘ˋ | ˘ˋ | ˘ˋ.

2. "What help for those who grimly close us out": The same can be said of this line. It is possible to hear an accent on the "us" which

separates "close" and "out" and to hear one on the "what" that starts the line. If you do hear them, then we have initial and final spondees. Spondees are the most common variations in iambic meter. They give us accents where we expect them, so they produce little disturbance. The line is a bit denser because of them. The spondee at the beginning of the line seems more plausible than the one at the end because "what" and "help" have similar strengths, but "us" is weaker than "close" and the metrical stress points toward "out." The metrical expectation of the pattern also points toward "help," so we opt for scanning it as a regular iambic line, but putting a spondee at the beginning is certainly justifiable.

3. "to prove some point or recompense unkind?": The three unaccented syllables imply that there may be a metrical accent here. What we hear is a secondary accent on "recompense." The word is accented on the first syllable: "RE-compense." But there is a secondary accent on "-PENSE." Try reading the line that way. It works, but only in this environment.

4. "When we speak, I feel some mirror-light": This line is one syllable short. Count them: there are nine. What's happened is that either the first or last foot has been shortened to a monosyllabic foot; this is called **catalexis**. The term can be applied to a truncation at the end of the line or at the beginning. You could read this as a trochaic line with a **catalectic** fifth foot. But if you consider the prevailing meter so far and decide the catalectic foot is the first one, then an iambic pattern emerges. We get all iambs except for the first foot. A monosyllabic foot must be an accent. This gives us an iambic pentameter line with an incomplete first foot, that is, with a monosyllabic foot substituted for an iamb.

5. "my ancient self, come back to haunt me now": There is nothing to note here except that once again the pronoun is not accented. The accents are on "back" and "haunt"—words that carry more significance than "me."

6. "No word is word enough. No touch or look": This is another perfectly straightforward line. It is possible to accent the first "No" for rhetorical reasons, and read the first foot as a spondee, but the metrical impulse tends to override this consideration for us. You may hear it differently.

7. "suffices. My fingers lengthen like a shadow": Here we do have a few problems or rather complications. For one thing the last unaccented syllable is part of a rather strange rhyme. The unaccented syl-

lable "-ow" in "SHAD-ow" rhymes with "now." It's traditional to simply forget about unaccented syllables at the ends of iambic lines, but this one conveys the rhyme and is a little harder to forget. The metrical accent in this line is on "like," which is the middle syllable of three unaccented syllables. Try it and you'll see it works well. But there is a substitution toward the beginning of the line. The end of "suffices," a three-syllable word with the accent in the middle, is unaccented, as is the "my" in the phrase "my fingers." We don't really expect an accent here. If they were someone else's fingers, then maybe there would be an accent, but "my" is expected. That means that the line starts with an iamb, which is followed by an anapest. There are various ways to interpret the effect. Sometimes an anapestic substitution makes a line seem a bit prosier, more natural. Sometimes it helps emphasize the first accent; here, "FING-ers."

8. "and grip an empty sleeve, or stop a book": This line is in regular iambs.

9. "His funeral gets larger every day": The metrical accent here is the very mild, secondary accent in "funeral." Since the first syllable is accented, the only possible secondary accent is on the third syllable, "funer-AL." With that taken care of, the line is perfectly iambic.

10. "her eyes have entered his blankest photographs": Again in this line we have a metrical stress on a secondary accent. The word "photographs" is accented on the first syllable; however, the third syllable can receive a slight emphasis—try it. It picks up the alternating pattern. The other place in which two unaccented syllables appear is in the passage "entered his blankest." The accent on "BLANK-est" is very strong. That means we'd have a hard time justifying one on "his" and, as is so often the case with pronouns that don't surprise, we can't here. So we have the substitution of an anapest in the third foot. You may have noted that there are a number of anapestic substitutions in this poem. It seems to be part of the style. It may be that Powell is trying to make the poem seem more conversational, more like the sister's actual speech.

11. "She doesn't see mother, father, or me": The question in this line is how to pronounce "doesn't?" Is it, as the apostrophe seems to indicate, "doznt," or is it "DOZ-ent?" Powell seems to hear the latter. Reading that way, we have two iambs, followed by two trochees, followed by an iamb. The effect is an emphasis on "mother" and "father," before we return to the regular scheme with "me."

12. "A broken doll, she looks at our tears, and laughs": This line

has eleven syllables, one more than the typical iambic-pentameter line; this suggests an anapest is present. The second to the last foot with two unaccented syllables is an anapest.

13. "A ghost between us parts our common air—": This line is regular.

14. "immune to love, logic, our hardest prayers": The line looks regular except for the third foot. The word "logic" is a trochee. Once we see that, we can see that the rest of the line is regular. Emphasis is achieved by using a reversed foot, and is further enhanced by alliteration. Love and logic may be the implied ends of a scale. If you can't be reached by either love or logic, how can you be reached?

The poem is clearly written in iambic pentameter. But the meter has been loosened up a bit, as Frost might say, to make it sound more like a speaking voice. Most of that loosening has been accomplished by substitutions, primarily anapestic substitutions. There are some trochaic substitutions as well, generally to heighten or emphasize contrasts. The poem moves along nicely on its rhythmic pulse, with enough variation to keep it from getting too predictable or singsong. But there is never any doubt that this is a metrical poem and capable of those sorts of rhythmic underlinings only metrical poems can achieve.

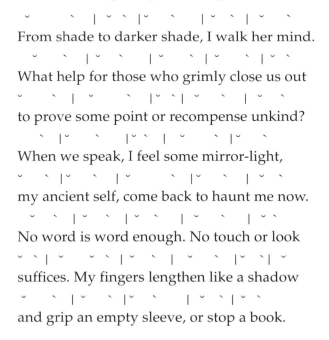

ˇ ` |ˇ `| ˇ `|ˇ `|ˇ `
His funeral gets larger every day:

ˇ ` | ˇ `| ˇ ˇ ` |ˇ `|ˇ `
her eyes have entered his blankest photographs.

ˇ ` |ˇ ` | ` ˇ |` ˇ |ˇ `
She doesn't see mother, father, or me.

ˇ `| ˇ ` | ˇ ` |ˇ ˇ ` |ˇ `
A broken doll, she looks at our tears, and laughs.

ˇ ` | ˇ ` |ˇ ` | ˇ ` | ˇ `
A ghost between us parts our common air—

ˇ ` | ˇ ` |` ˇ |ˇ ` |ˇ `
immune to love, logic, our hardest prayers.

4 More Observations about Metrical Terms

You have probably noticed that after we mark the syllables in a line with accent and unaccent marks and then put in virgules to mark feet, the feet do not always correspond to words. This can be confusing. Often you are given an example like the following:

> "Between" is a two-syllable word (be•tween), accented on the second syllable (be-TWEEN); it can be considered iambic. On the other hand "access," also a two syllable word (ac•cess), is accented on the first syllable, (AC-cess), and is thus a trochee.

Nonetheless, it's not words, but combinations of syllables that form feet. Sometimes the combination of syllables may be a word. Just as frequently, it is not. A foot can include the end of one word and the beginning of another.

If the feet in a line are chiefly anapests, then we say the line is anapestic. Likewise, if the dominant foot is the iamb, we say the line is iambic. This does not mean every foot in the line is an iamb. There may be other sorts, called **substitutions**, because they are *in the places of* iambs. The most common substitutions are trochees and spondees for iambs. Poets may use extra unaccented syllables in the middle of the line or at the end, but these are not significant variations. The extra syllable in rhyme words is not fussed over because English is a rhyme-poor language—unlike Italian or French—and exact monosyllabic rhymes are hard to find. This is one of the reasons twentieth-century poets have experimented with types of rhyme; they wanted to undermine the predictability inherent in particular rhyme words. They have invented terms like *slant, off, half,* or *near* rhymes to describe how far away from perfect rhyme they were willing to go. Perfect rhyme can be either monosyllabic or polysyllabic; for example, these are full rhymes: fat/sat, dreaming/scheming; kodiak/zodiak; pelican/belly can. We won't try to distinguish between a slant and a near rhyme, but modern poets using these same rhyme words might have chosen these connections: fat/great; dreaming/thinking; Kodiak/cognac; pelican/garbage can. Some poets, such as W. H. Auden, have even experimented with rhyming the accented syllable in a **falling rhyme** with the accented syllable in a **ris-**

ing rhyme, so *ocean* would be rhymed with *below*; the variations have gotten rather intricate.

Until recently, rhymes that ended softly, with an unaccented syllable (in words like *pleasure, double, talents)*, were called "feminine rhymes," and those that ended strongly, "masculine rhymes," but many feminist scholars objected to what appeared to be a sexist distinction. However, these terms were invented by troubadour poets and referred only to grammatical gender. The *New Princeton Encyclopedia of Poetry and Poetics* says that "both terms derived from the declension of adjectives in Occitan, but they long survived the decay of the inflectional systems of Old French and Medieval English as purely technical terms in prosody, so that they now have nothing to do with grammatical gender" (1993, 737). Occitan was that region in southern France where Languedoc and Old Provençal were spoken. Word endings in the Occitan language indicated grammatical gender, but that language no longer exists—at least in its original form. Yet in an effort to understand the present meanings for masculine and feminine word endings, we tend to see them as sexist—"soft" versus "strong." So there is a need to update the terms. Alternatives have been suggested, such as **rising** and **falling rhymes**, although this can cause confusion with **rising** and **falling rhythm**.

For our purposes, words with accented endings like "prevent" (˘ ´) or "delay" (˘ ´) are said to be "rising" while words with unaccented endings like "borrow" (´ ˘) or "happy" (´ ˘) are said to be falling. This distinction isn't particularly important except that the falling syllables at the ends of iambic lines are often ignored. Also, lines in trochaic meters frequently end with an incomplete foot, as do these from Blake's "The Tyger":

>   ´ ˘ | ´ ˘ | ´   ˘ | ´
> Tyger, tyger burning bright,
>
>   ´ ˘ | ´ ˘ | ´   ˘ | ´
> In the forests of the night.

The last foot is missing an unaccented syllable, but in trochaic meters this is one of the primary uses of the monosyllabic foot. In fact, it is such a common strategy that the word **catalexis** is used to describe the omission. We would say that the fourth foot in Blake's poem is **catalectic** (this adjectival form refers specifically to the omission of one syllable, and catalexis refers to any shortening at the beginning or end of a line).

5 Meter among Us

Calculating the meter in a phrase, line, or sentence is generally the province of poets, but prose writers also have a sense of meter in their heads. They would rather call it rhythm. For them rhythm is bound up in voice, tone, and pacing (the general movement or development of the story). Many of the best prose writers, like William Faulkner and James Joyce, started out writing poems and brought this attachment to the syllable to their prose. As a brief illustration, consider this stanza from an early Joyce poem called "She Weeps over Rahoon":

> Rain on Rahoon falls softly, softly falling
> Where my dark lover lies.
> Sad is his voice that calls me, sadly calling
> At grey moonrise.

The poem ends with a description of the dead lover's heart as having "lain under the moon-grey nettles, / The black mould and muttering rain."

Now compare these lines with one of his most famous and beautiful scenes from the last story in *Dubliners,* called "The Dead," where Gabriel considers his wife's first love, Michael Furey, who died after having stood too long in the rain waiting for her:

> Snow was general all over Ireland. It was falling on every part of the dark central plain, on the treeless hills, falling softly upon the Bog of Allen and, farther westward, softly falling into the dark mutinous Shannon waves. It was falling, too, upon every part of the lonely churchyard on the hill where Michael Furey lay buried. It lay thickly drifted on the crooked crosses and headstones, on the spears of the little gate, on the barren thorns. His soul swooned slowly as he heard the snow falling faintly through the universe and faintly falling, like the descent of their last end, upon all the living and the dead. (1968, 223–24)

These sentences are very metrical. There is a rhythmic mixture of iambs, trochees, anapests, and spondees. Joyce has applied what he discovered in his poetry to his prose. He uses spondees to slow down the action, to bunch or gather the line and give it some tension.

In the poem there are three stresses in a row in the first line: "-hoon," "falls," and "soft-." This slows down the action, as if the rain were slowly accumulating in this pause. The repetition and inversion of *soft* and *fall* illustrate the effect of continuous, but slightly varied action and imply that Gabriel's emotions go through a sequence of related stages while he watches the snow. The meaning in the two passages is strikingly similar, too. In each, a lover has died and the observer contemplates the rain or snow falling on the grave. The second sentence of the poem—the third line—begins with an accented syllable, creating a trochee, which is followed by an iamb; this creates the sliding effect of an anapest. The sadness slides into the voice, and this repetition—"calls me, sadly calling"—echoes the "falls softly, softly falling" above. The echo becomes part of the voice and dramatizes the sadness. One might argue that this is emotional manipulation, a romantic indulgence that the reader is told to participate in without really knowing anything about the man who has died, and that the writer is exploiting the death of a loved one to gain emotional depth. Another might argue that it is merely a lyrical expression, a plain statement of the speaker's feelings, and to criticize it is to be a little unfeeling, unsympathetic. Certainly, in the story, all the information is supplied and the effect is dramatic and affecting.

Spondees have the effect of stopping the action, building tension, creating a spot of anguish in the line. The spondees in the prose— "dark cent-," "dark mut-," "churchyard," "lay thick-" and "headstones"—have this effect. The anapests have a graceful sweep and are often used to illustrate dance rhythms. They are occasionally used after spondees to give the end a kind of sweeping and grand closure. This is the effect after "headstones": "on the spears of the little gate, on the barren thorns"—two anapests followed by an iamb followed by an anapest and a final iamb. It is like a waltz in which two long strides are followed by one that regains stability, another stride, a final firm step. Yet the next sentence stops us completely with three long accented syllables in a row: "soul," "swooned," and "slow-." It would be interesting to look at the meter of that whole sentence:

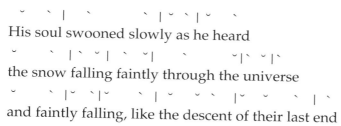

His soul swooned slowly as he heard

the snow falling faintly through the universe

and faintly falling, like the descent of their last end

˘ ` | ` ˘ | ` ˘ | ` ˘ | `
upon all the living and the dead.

The meter in the last four sentences of the story is very regular and poem-like. This occurs right after the prosaic reference to the newspaper account: "Yes, the newspapers were right: snow was general all over Ireland." The following "poem" is designed to provide an emotional contrast to all that is daily and mundane. We broke this last sentence into phrases according to the slight pauses we would make if we were to read it aloud. Even the texture of the language is compelling. There are end rhymes—"heard," "end," "dead"—and the "s" sounds slide up against the "d" sounds as if the swoon is beset by hard conclusions. The assonance (the "o" and "a" and "e" sounds, especially) and **consonance** (the "f" and "l," especially) create a multilayered texture that matches the emotion beautifully. This is a very well-orchestrated dance, and Joyce pulls our hearts along with him by carefully modulating his meter. He could not have done this so skillfully without having written poetry first; in fact it is clear that he reused what he discovered in his poem to create one of the most lovely and poetic passages in English literature.

It should be clear, then, that the uses of metrical language are not confined to poems, though poems are meter's primary habitat. In oral poetry, meter was used as a memory aid as well as a generative tool. Homer's *Iliad* was created in a time when writing soon disappeared into what has been called a Greek Dark Age. The *Iliad* is 15,593 lines of hexameter. The original *Iliad* may not have been as long: some maintain that through centuries of improvisation and serial retelling by gifted storytellers it achieved its final form. As Milman Parry, an American scholar, has pointed out, these improvisational storytellers had a reservoir of epithets to use when the meter in a particular line demanded it. For example, an Achaean—a soldier from a Greek tribe that occupied the northern portion of the Peloponnesus—could be described as "longhaired," "strong-greaved," or "bronze-cloaked" (1971, quoted in Knox 1990, 15). Each of these in the original Greek had a different metrical structure and could fit into the beginning, middle, or end of the line. The six feet in the Homeric line were very structured. Bernard Knox, in his introduction to Robert Fagles's translation, describes it this way: "This is a line . . . which may, to put it crudely, be either dactyls . . . or spondees . . . in the first four places but must be dactyl and spondee in that order in the last two (rarely spondee and spondee, never spondee followed by a dactyl) . . . and unlike most English verse, the meter does not allow departures from basic norms" (1990, 12). Regardless of whether Homer actually wrote it all or had help, something written in a steady predictable rhythm is easier to remember than a more random arrangement of syllables. Also, the epithets or predictable pieces of description gave the raconteur time to conceive of the next line or phrase. If we stopped to examine the lines we have memorized, we would probably discover a fairly regular metrical flow.

Metrical regularity is also used in advertising jingles, nursery rhymes, children's hand-slapping games, and jump-rope songs because of this sticking power—even when we don't want them to stick. The goal of advertisers is to implant a bit of language in our heads so that it hums in there when we pass their products with a grocery cart. Here's an old one that was very effective: "Raid Kills Bugs Dead." It is two spondees or four stressed syllables in a row without any relief. It is like four little gavel taps, and the d's act as a frame or parentheses around them, giving the phrase a sense of closure and enclosure. The obvious redundancy lightens the heavy syllables a little, makes them seem like a smirk; the steady forward position of the mouth and tongue as we say each word makes the phrase seem like a taunt. A slogan like "Always Coca-Cola" presents three equal trochees in a row. The soda name itself is clever: there is something reassuring about repetition with a slight variation: Coca-cola, heebee jeebees, cobbly wobbly, haberdasher. It is a kind of distorted mirror-rhyme. There is also something insidiously addicting about these rhyming doubles, these mental pirouettes our heads seem to enjoy without the sanction of the will. For example, remember this mind-worm? "Bounty is the quicker picker-upper." There are five regular trochees in a row and the internal mirror-rhyme wriggles it deeper into our heads.

Another example of this is from the Doublemint gum commercial: "Double your pleasure, double your fun / with double-good, double-fresh, Doublemint gum." The repetition of the word "double" and its slight variation into "Doublemint" create that mirror effect, and the meter slithers its way into our unwilling heads. The first line has four feet—trochee, iamb, iamb, anapest. The trochee juxtaposed with the iamb creates the effect of an anapest, and the sliding anapests in the line account for the dancing, rollicking gait and another kind of mirror effect. The second line has five feet—iamb, spondee, iamb, trochee, and spondee. The verbal effect is a kind of dance-ending where the dancer does a little stylistic flourish and extends his arm graciously to his partner—in this case, gum. It is a quick-drying bit of mind adhesive, which is very hard to remove once it's been attached.

The power of the spondee can be seen in this line from a McDonald's commercial: "Two all-beef patties special sauce / lettuce cheese pickles onions on a sesame-seed bun." The interplay of iambs and trochees, which create knots or spondees in the line, has the effect of a jump-rope or hand-clapping game. The dominant rhythm is iambic, but the spondees like "beef/pat-" and "cheese/pick-" and "seed/bun" are hand-slapping opportunities.

Jump-rope songs are especially good illustrations of the spondee's effect. Here is one that you will probably recognize:

` ˘ | ` ˘ | ` ˘ | ` ˘
Father, Father, call the doctor

` ˘ | ` ˘ | ` ˘ | ` ˘
Momma has a new-born baby.

˘ ` | ˘ ˘ ` | ˘ ` | ˘ ˘ `
It isn't a boy, it isn't a girl

˘ ` | ˘ ` | ˘ ` | ˘
It's just a plain old baby.

` ˘ | ` ˘ | ` ˘ | ` ˘
Send it down the elevator

` ˘ | ` ˘ | ` ˘ | ` ˘
Wrap it up in tissue paper

` ` | ` or
` ˘ | `
First floor stop

` ˘ | ` ` or
` ˘ ˘ | `
Second floor stop

` ` | ` ˘ | ` ˘ | ` or
` ˘ | ˘ ˘ ` | ˘ `
Third floor kick it out the door.

The shorter and more consistently metrical the line, the faster it moves. The first two lines are trochaic tetrameter, and the repetition of "Father" sets up an urgent tone and a chantlike quality. The rope slaps the ground at each stress, and the unstressed syllables provide breathing room. The spondees in the last three lines are clear stops, suggesting the end of the turn. The three stresses in the last line are indeed a "kick" out of the song and the twirling jump rope; the two iambs at the end relieve the tension and give the jumper a place to go. This is much more gentle than ending on a spondee like "mint/gum" above, and we are returned to the atmosphere of a game rather than the violent wishes of siblings who don't want to have to compete for their mother's and father's attention.

Children's verbal games must be metrically consistent. They depend upon being easily memorized and rhythmical—there are metrical substitutions, but they tend to facilitate speed. For example, "ring around the rosie a pocket full of posies" is a sequence of trochees and iambs, and the more regular they are, the more easily they enter our heads. Children can learn these rhymes after hearing them once or twice. Nonsense syllables have to be very regular; otherwise, we can't remember them at all. Here is an example of a hand-slapping nonsense verse: "Zig, zig, zig / eenie weenie what's a beenie / op hop bop-a-teenie / ootchi-cootchi Liberace / I love you tootie frootie." The triple stresses (spondee variations) are double-slaps, and the accents like "een-" and "ween-" are single crossover slaps. These are similar to where the jump rope hits the ground in the jump-rope rhymes.

The point is, we all have metrical language in our heads, whether we recognize it or not. We have all listened and responded to it for years. What we are asking you to do in this book is to pay attention to something you already know quite a bit about. It is true that poets use meter much more subtly than the writers of nursery rhymes, jump-rope songs, and advertisers, but you already have a feeling for meter and know something about its general effects. Hearing meter is just a matter of listening closely to sounds you hear every day. Once you start paying attention to meter, you can make your own writing more effective and analyze just how a beautiful passage achieved its beauty.

However, we must warn you, this can become an addicting habit, perhaps even an annoying tic. Sometimes we catch ourselves scanning what people say, especially if there was an overtly metrical phrase in the sentence. People might begin to wonder about your pensive silences.

6 Types of Metrical Lines

As we have said, the metrical designation for a line in accentual-syllabic meter has a two-part name. The first part indicates the foot (iambic, trochaic, dactylic, etc.) while the second part indicates the number of feet in the line. We use Greek and Latin prefixes to indicate metrical line lengths, so the standard English meters are **monometer** (one foot), **dimeter** (two), **trimeter** (three), **tetrameter** (four), **pentameter** (five), **hexameter** (six), **heptameter** (seven). Let's start with stanzas that are written in a single meter. Examples of different length lines follow.

Monometer

This is the rarest form because the poet has so little room to move; it is like writing a poem on a strip of litmus paper—errors and clumsy moves show up rather quickly and obviously. Robert Herrick, who enjoyed the challenge of using a variety of meters and sound effects, wrote this poem in iambic monometer:

Thus I

Pass by

And die

Alone

Unknown

And gone.

Dimeter

Dimeter is most often used in **complex stanza** forms, but can be found, if uncommonly, as the exclusive meter of a poem. Here is an example from Thomas Wyatt, from a poem called "What Should I Say."

$$\breve{} \quad \grave{} \quad | \breve{} \quad \grave{} \quad \text{ or}$$
$$\grave{} \quad \breve{} \quad | \breve{} \quad \grave{}$$

What should I say,

$$\breve{} \quad \grave{} \quad | \quad \breve{} \quad \grave{}$$

Since faith is dead,

$$\breve{} \quad \grave{} \quad | \breve{} \quad \grave{}$$

And truth away

$$\breve{} \quad \grave{} \quad | \quad \breve{} \quad \grave{}$$

From you is fled?

$$\breve{} \quad \grave{} | \breve{} \quad \grave{}$$

Should I be led

$$\breve{} \quad \grave{} \quad | \breve{} \quad \grave{}$$

With doubleness?

$$\grave{} \quad \grave{} \quad | \quad \grave{} \quad \breve{}$$

Nay, nay, Mistress!

You might notice that "doubleness" is part of the theme here. The last line contains two substitutions: a spondee followed by a trochee. The effect is a double emphasis.

The best-known example of dactylic dimeter is Thomas Hood's "The Bridge of Sighs," from which the following is taken.

$$\grave{} \quad \breve{} \quad \breve{} \quad | \quad \grave{} \quad \breve{} \quad \breve{}$$

Touch her not scornfully;

$$\grave{} \quad \breve{} \quad \breve{} \quad | \quad \grave{} \quad \breve{} \quad \breve{}$$

Think of her mournfully,

$$\grave{} \quad \breve{} \quad \breve{} \quad | \quad \grave{} \quad \breve{} \quad \breve{}$$

Gently and humanly;

$$\grave{} \quad \breve{} \quad \breve{} \quad | \quad \grave{} \quad \breve{} \quad \breve{}$$

Not of the stains of her,

$$\grave{} \quad \breve{} \quad \breve{} | \grave{} \quad \breve{} \quad \breve{}$$

All that remains of her

` ˘ ˘ | ` ˘ ˘
Now is pure womanly.

Trimeter

Trimeter is a fairly common meter, associated with light songs. Here is the opening of John Clare's "Come Hither," which is in iambic trimeter.

˘ ` | ˘ ` | ˘ `
Come hither, ye who thirst;

` ` | ˘ ` | ˘ `   or
` ` | ˘ ` | ` `
Pure still the brook flows on;

˘ ` | ˘ ` | ˘ `
Its waters are not cursed;

` ˘ | ˘ ` | ˘ `
Clear from its rocks of stone

˘ ` | ˘ ` | ˘ `
It bubbles and it boils,

˘ ` | ˘ ` | ˘ `
An everlasting rill,

˘ ` | ˘ ` | ˘ `
Then eddies and recoils

˘ ` | ˘ ` | ˘ `
And wimples clearer still.

` ` | ˘ ` | ˘ ` | ˘   or
` ` | ˘ ` | ` ` | ˘
Art troubled? then come hither,

˘ ` | ˘ ` | ˘ ` | ˘
And taste of peace forever.

But it can become more serious as in this well-known short poem by A. E. Housman called "With Rue My Heart Is Laden."

˘ ` | ˘ ` | ˘ ` | ˘
With rue my heart is laden

˘ ` | ˘ ` | ˘ `
For golden friends I had,

˘ ˎ | ˘ ˘ ˎ | ˘ ˎ | ˘   or
˘ ˎ | ˘ ˘ ˎ | ˘ ˎ ˎ | ˘

For many a rose-lipt maiden

˘   ˎ | ˘ ˘ ˎ | ˘ ˎ   ˎ   or
˘   ˎ | ˘ ˘ ˎ | ˘ ˎ   ˎ

And many a lightfoot lad.

˘   ˎ | ˘   ˎ | ˘ ˎ | ˘

By brooks too broad for leaping

˘   ˎ | ˘   ˎ | ˘ ˎ   ˎ   or
˘   ˎ | ˘ ˎ   ˎ | ˘ ˎ   ˎ

The lightfoot boys are laid;

˘   ˎ | ˘   ˎ | ˘ ˎ   ˎ | ˘   or
˘   ˎ | ˘ ˎ   ˎ | ˘ ˎ   ˎ | ˘

The rose-lipt girls are sleeping

˘   ˎ | ˘   ˘ ˎ | ˘ ˎ

In fields where roses fade.

Tetrameter

Tetrameter is one of the two most common measures in English poetry. Here's Mark Halperin's "The Alarm."

˘ ˎ | ˘ ˘ ˎ | ˘   ˘ ˎ | ˘ ˎ   ˎ

A faulty burglar alarm goes off

˘   ˎ | ˘   ˎ | ˘ ˎ | ˘   ˎ

and you, still coiled in sleep my friend,

ˎ | ˘ ˘ | ˘   ˎ | ˘ ˎ

rise to dial the manager.

˘ ˎ | ˘ ˘ | ˘   ˎ | ˘ ˎ

Police arrive. And in the end

˘   ˎ | ˘   ˎ | ˘ ˎ | ˘   ˎ

we all crawl back to bed. Four times—

ˎ   ˘ | ˘   ˎ | ˘ ˘ | ˘   ˎ

then, on the fifth, I hear your screams:

ˎ ˎ | ˘ ˎ | ˎ   ˎ | ˘ ˎ

my lawyer will call yours. Rocks

˘   ` | ˘    ` | ˘   ` | ˘       `
will smash the windows of your dreams.

˘   `  | ˘    ` | ˘   ` | ˘˘
Your anger sings. The singleness

˘   ` | ˘    ` | `    ˘ | ˘   `
you wanted most flees, to return

`   ˘    | ˘   ` | ˘   ` |  ˘    ˘   `
altered and in control. The alarm,

˘   `        | ˘ ` | ` ` ` | ˘    `
the damned alarm rings on and on.

Pentameter

Pentameter is the most common meter in English poetry. Most sonnets are written in this meter, and so is **blank verse**—the chosen form for Shakespeare's plays and John Milton's *Paradise Lost*. Here is the **octet** from Robert Frost's sonnet called "Design." (Sonnets are fourteen lines; the first eight lines are often called an **octet**, and the last six, a **sestet**.)

˘   `   | ˘   ` | ˘   ` | ˘    ` | ˘   `
I found a dimpled spider, fat and white,

`   ˘ |  `   `   | ˘    ` | ˘   ` | ˘    `   or
˘   ˘ | `     ` | ˘   ` | ˘    ` | ˘   `
On a white heal-all, holding up a moth

`     ˘ |  `   `  | ˘  ` | ˘ ` | ˘    `   or
˘   ˘ | `     ` | ˘ ` | ˘  ` | ˘   `
Like a white piece of rigid satin cloth—

˘   ` | ˘    ` | ˘ ` | ˘    ` | ˘   `
Assorted characters of death and blight

`       ` | ˘ ` | ˘    ` | ˘   ` | ˘       `
Mixed ready to begin the morning right,

`    ˘ | ˘  ˘ | ˘ ` | ˘ ˘ ` | ˘        `
Like the ingredients of a witches' broth—

˘   `  | ˘     ` | ˘ ˘ ` | ˘   ` | ˘ `   or
˘   `  | ˘     ` | ˘ ˘ ` | ˘   ` | ˘ `
A snow-drop spider, a flower like a froth,

˘   `  | `   ` | ˘  ` | ˘ ` | ˘    `
And dead wings carried like a paper kite.

Notice that there are six variations in only eight lines. Too much regularity in the pentameter line can force the rhythm into a singsong pattern. Most poets who are writing serious poems try to counter this effect with variations.

Hexameter

Hexameter was used by Homer in the *Iliad* and *Odyssey*, and this meter has been imitated in translations of those poems. It also appears as part of some fixed stanza forms like the **Spenserian stanza**. When it appears in these forms it is called an *alexandrine,* as we noted earlier. Here's an example of iambic hexameter by Edward Thomas, from his poem "Melancholy":

> ˘ `  | ˘  ` | ˘ `  | ˘  ` | `  ` | ˘ `
> The rain and wind, the rain and wind, raved endlessly.

> ˘ `  | ˘  ` | ˘ `  | ˘  `| ˘ ˘ `  |˘  ` |˘
> On me the Summer storm, and fever, and melancholy

> `  ` |˘ `  | ˘  `|˘ `  | ˘  ` |˘ `
> Wrought magic, so that if I feared the solitude

> ˘ `  |˘  ` |˘ `  |˘ ` |˘ `  | ˘  `
> Far more I feared all company: too sharp, too rude,

> ˘ `  | ˘  ` |˘ `|˘  ` |˘ `  | ˘  `
> Had been the wisest or the dearest human voice.

> ˘ `| ˘  ` |˘ `  |˘  ` | ˘ `  |˘        `   or
> ˘ `| ˘  ` |˘ `  | ˘  ` | ˘ `  | ˘        `
> What I desired I knew not, but whate'er my choice

> `  ˘| ˘  ` | ˘ `  |˘  ` | ˘ `  | ˘  `
> Vain it must be, I knew. Yet naught did my despair

> ˘   `  | ˘  ˘  ` | ˘ `  | ˘  ` | ˘   `  | `   or
> ˘   `  | ˘  ˘  | `   `  | ˘  ` | ˘   ˘ | `    `
> But sweeten the strange sweetness, while through the wild air

> ˘ ˘ | `  ˘  `| `  ˘  `| ˘ `  | ` ˘ ` | ˘   or
> `  |`   `  |˘  ` | ˘ `  | ˘  ˘  | ` ˘ | `  ` | ˘
> All day long I heard a distant cuckoo calling

> ˘ `  |˘  ` |˘ `  | ` ˘ ˘ | `  ` | ˘ `| ˘
> And, soft as dulcimers, sounds of near water falling,

˘　　ˋ　|　˘　　ˋ　|　˘　ˋ　|　˘　ˋ|　ˋ|˘　ˋ
And, softer, and remote as if in history,

ˋ　　˘　|˘　　ˋ　|　˘　　ˋ　　|　˘　　ˋ　|　˘　　ˋ　|˘　ˋ
Rumors of what had touched my friends, my foes, or me.

Heptameter

Heptameter is seen by many as merely a combination of tetrameter and trimeter—if two such lines were joined, they would form a heptameter line. Nonetheless, there are poems written in heptameter. Here is the opening stanza of Thomas Hardy's "Wessex Heights."

˘　　ˋ　|　˘　　　ˋ　|˘　　ˋ|　˘　　　ˋ　|˘ˋ|˘　˘　ˋ　|˘　ˋ
There are some heights in Wessex, shaped as if by a kindly hand

˘　ˋ　|˘　　ˋ　|　˘　ˋ|˘　ˋ|　˘　　˘　ˋ|˘　　ˋ　|˘　ˋ
For thinking, dreaming, dying on, and at crises when I stand,

˘　˘　ˋ|˘　　ˋ|˘　　ˋ|　˘　ˋ|˘　　ˋ|˘　ˋ　|˘　ˋ
Say, on Ingpen Beacon eastward, or on Wylls-Neck westwardly,

˘　ˋ　|　˘　˘　ˋ|˘ˋ|˘　　ˋ　|　˘　ˋ|˘　　ˋ　|˘　ˋ
I seem where I was before my birth, and after death may be.

About Complex Stanza Forms

We have considered poems written in single meters, but some stanzas are more complex and have lines of different lengths. It is easy to describe such stanzas using this system. You need only say how many lines the stanza consists of and then name the line length of each line or group of lines. For example, monometer usually appears in a stanza having lines of other lengths. John Donne's "Song" is in trochaic tetrameter except for the seventh and eighth lines, which are in iambic monometer. Donne often used many variations, and as a consequence, his meters were considered rough by his critics. Here's the first stanza:

ˋ　˘　|　ˋ　˘|　ˋ　˘|　ˋ
Go and catch a falling star.

ˋ　˘　|　ˋ　˘|　ˋ　˘　|　ˋ
Get with child a mandrake root.

ˋ　˘|　ˋ　　˘|　ˋ　　ˋ　|　ˋ　　or
ˋ　˘|　ˋ　　ˋ|　ˋ　　ˋ　|　ˋ
Tell me where all past years are,

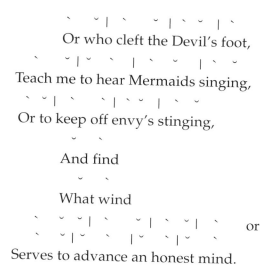

Or who cleft the Devil's foot,

Teach me to hear Mermaids singing,

Or to keep off envy's stinging,

And find

What wind

    or

Serves to advance an honest mind.

7 Syllabic or Strong-Stress Meters

Traditional English meter is called **accentual-syllabic** because it combines the elements of two other systems. In Japanese all syllables receive equal stress. Most Romance languages like French, Spanish, and Italian have fixed stresses, but they are lighter than in Germanic languages like German, English, Norwegian, Danish, and Swedish, or in Slavic languages such as Russian and Polish. In both Japanese and the Romance languages, line length is determined by syllable count. For example, the alexandrine in French poetry is a twelve-syllable line. It is common to talk of octosyllabic and decasyllabic lines, lines of eight and ten syllables. Although these terms have been applied to English poetry, it is a borrowing that has often led to misunderstandings. But there have been poets writing in English who have experimented with a kind of **quantitative verse—syllabic verse.** In syllabic verse the measure is determined by the number of syllables in a line. English syllables have a broad range: a word like "var-i-able" has three syllables, but the second is very short; words like "strength" or "traipsed" are long, full sounds. This lack of uniformity makes the syllable an inconsistent unit of measurement, so it has not been a popular form in English. Marianne Moore, one of the great twentieth-century poets, wrote poems that sounded like prose, but were actually carefully measured syllables, and rhymed. Others have written successful syllabic verse as well. Consider this poem with lines of nine syllables by Thom Gunn. It is called "Rastignac at 45."

> Here he is of course. It was his best
> trick always: when we glance again toward
> the shadow we see it has consist-
> ed of him all along, lean and bored.
> We denounced him so often! Yet he
> comes up, and leans on one of the bars
> in his dark suit, indicating the
> empty glass as if we were waiters.

Although some listeners claim to be able to "hear" these measures, there is serious doubt whether this is actually the case. So why write in syllabics? The regularity challenges the poet, makes him or her stretch. As Auden wrote, "Blessed be all metrical rules that forbid automatic responses . . . " (1976, 642).

Even less common than syllabics, but with deeper roots in the history of prosody, is the use of **accentuals**—a verse form that employs a fixed number of accents to the line, regardless of the number of syllables. Anglo-Saxon poems were written in lines that consisted of two halves, **hemistiches**, each of which had two accents that were marked by **alliteration**. Thus, a full line had four accents. The spaces between these accents were of varying lengths, but it's believed the poems were chanted with harp accompaniment; the accented syllables were meant to coincide with the beats of the music. In this system, strong stress was emphasized, but the syllable count was inconsequential.

This method found few practitioners after the Middle Ages. By the time Geoffrey Chaucer started to write at the end of the fourteenth century, the character of English had undergone major transformations. An enormous number of French words had come into English, and the innovations of French prosody were also imported. William Langland's accentual *Piers Plowman,* written in the late 1300s, is a sort of nostalgic leftover, as are the experiments of John Skelton (a late fifteenth- to early sixteenth-century poet whose contribution to poetry has become known as **skeltonics**: lines of two or three stresses whose end rhyme usually repeats in couplets but can go on for three or four lines). Something like accentual poetry was revived or hinted at in the poems of Gerard Manley Hopkins, but these were unknown until the twentieth century. Ezra Pound experimented with it in his translations. The best-known modern examples of strong stress or accentual poetry are by Richard Wilbur. Here are a few lines from his poem called "Junk," which bears an **epigraph** from *Waldere,* a late tenth- or early eleventh-century fragment of a poem (sixty-three lines survive) which was found in 1860 (it had been used as padding for another book's cover). This fragment was written in the form Wilbur's poem imitates. We have only marked the accents, for the unaccented syllables are not counted; notice that three of the four accents are alliterated.

An axe angles

From my neighbor's ashcan;

It is hell's handiwork,

the wood not hickory,

The flow of the grain

not faithfully followed.

The shivered shaft

rises from the shellheap

Of plastic playthings,

paper plates,

And the sheer shards

of shattered tumblers

That were not annealed

for the time needful.

8 More Metrical Analysis: Five Poems

Read the following poems and try to understand them before you start your scansion. The analysis of rhetorical stresses will not make much sense unless you do. Scan each poem before you go on to read our reasons for scanning the way we do. Be sure to check your scansion against the discussions that follow each poem.

A. **An Irish Airman Foresees His Death**, by W. B. Yeats

1. I know that I shall meet my fate
2. Somewhere among the clouds above;
3. Those that I fight I do not hate,
4. Those that I guard I do not love;
5. My country is Kiltartan Cross,
6. My countrymen Kiltartan's poor,
7. No likely end could bring them loss
8. Or leave them happier than before.
9. Nor law, nor duty bade me fight,
10. Nor public men, nor cheering crowds,
11. A lonely impulse of delight
12. Drove to this tumult in the clouds;
13. I balanced all, brought all to mind,
14. The years to come seemed waste of breath,
15. A waste of breath the years behind
16. In balance with this life, this death.

The basic metrical structure of this poem is iambic tetrameter, and the rhyming (abab) suggests **quatrains** that have been squeezed together. The effect of this compression is that the whole poem seems to come out of one mood, one tumbling and interlocking meditation. It is a pessimistic little poem whose pessimism is relieved by the Irish airman's one reason to live in an otherwise bleak landscape: his "lonely impulse of delight" while flying a plane. It is important to establish the **tone** because metrical changes will signal where the tone—and thus the meaning of the speaker—shifts.

1. "I know that I shall meet my fate": The rhetorical stresses in the first line are on "know," "meet," and "fate." We can plot these and

work with what remains. "Shall" is a strong syllable, and in a line like "I shall go home again," it is clearly stressed over a scrawny syllable like "I." We have already noted that subject pronouns are rarely stressed. We know who is speaking; we're most interested in what the speaker has to say. Thus, the accent is on "know." Note that there are two "I's", and they are stressed differently because of rhetorical considerations. By stressing the second "I," Yeats gives the reader a glimpse of what is to follow: a meditation on the private fate of the airman. There seems to be a stoical resignation in the blunt way the airman talks about his own death. Who will die in the clouds? I will. Here the sense is something like—not those people, but me—that's who will be dying! The speaker is stoical, but he is also proud.

2. "Somewhere among the clouds above": The greatest difficulty in scanning the second line is in the first foot; the other three feet are very clear and straightforward iambs. How do we scan "somewhere"? Both syllables are strong. The dictionary will tell us that the primary stress is on "some," but there is a secondary stress on "where." In fact, most of the "some-" words are that way: *someway, somewhat, sometime, somehow, someday, someone*; only *something* is shown without a secondary stress mark over the second syllable. Yeats is using either a trochee or a spondee in the first foot. Either one makes sense. If he heard a spondee, it isn't a loud one. It is a little gather or pleat in the sentence. The "somewhere" he's referring to is the place of his own death; there is a mild pause, a slight catch in the reflection here. One could also argue for the trochee: the stress on "some-" heightens the sense of vagueness, the sense that anywhere up there is as good as any other. Both arguments sound reasonable, and we wouldn't try to privilege one as better.

3. "Those that I fight I do not hate": The strongest syllables are "fight" and "hate"; the repetition of the "I" in "I fight I do" suggests that the metrical pattern is going to be the same—two iambs followed by a third. Both "I" and "do" are tiny syllables—a Lilliputian battle for importance—but "do" wins out; it gets a metrical stress. Now, back to the first two syllables. If you say them long enough, both words will probably sound stressed, but the rhetorical sense of the line heightens the importance of "those," as it does in line 4. Both "those" he hates and "those" he guards are the same; he literally puts them in the same position. Because we expect him to be more faithful to his countrymen, to patriotically love them more, it surprises us to find his enemies lumped together with his countrymen. The stress on "those" in lines 3 and 4

deliberately contradicts our expectation, and that is the speaker's intention because he wants to emphasize that his zeal for flying is not motivated by nationalism.

4. "Those that I guard I do not love": This is an echo of line 3, and "guard" and "love" operate like "fight" and "hate" above.

5. "My country is Kiltartan Cross": The only difficulty here is in knowing how to pronounce "Kiltartan"; the accent is on the second syllable. In the second metrical foot, "is" is weak, but it occurs between two similarly weak syllables ("-try" and "Kil-") and gets a metrical stress.

6. "My countrymen Kiltartan's poor": This line is scanned the same way as 5, but "men" gets a clear rhetorical stress, so this line should actually be easier to scan.

7. "No likely end could bring them loss": Each of the stressed syllables is clear: "like-," "end," "bring," and "loss." The only potential confusion is with "could," which may seem bigger than "end," but auxiliary verbs (as in line 1 with "shall") rarely take the stress over the verb unless the verb is weak, as in the line "it shall be done."

8. "Or leave them happier than before": The only difficulty is with a word like "happier." When you slow down, you notice that it has three syllables like the words *family, fluttering, dalliance, ivory, Julia*. Yet in conversation, we generally blur the second and third syllables because the second is small and dominated by a short vowel sound. We think that is what Yeats is doing. It is an old and common tactic—Shakespeare does it too. It is possible to see the third foot as an anapest, but there is no content justification for this, no obvious reason to include this variation except to make the line sound more like speech.

9 and 10. "Nor law, nor duty bade me fight, / Nor public men, nor cheering crowds": These are straightforward iambic tetrameter lines, and the lexical stresses help us plot the accents.

11. "A lonely impulse of delight": The only difficulty in this line is with the word "impulse." If you look it up in the dictionary you will find that it is like "somewhere" in line 2: both syllables in the word are stressed, but the major stress is on the first syllable. In two-syllable words, one syllable will dominate, unless it is a compound word like "bullpen" or "shotgun," and even then one syllable usually dominates. There are some words in our language whose accents shift when a suffix is added, which illustrates how tricky this business is. For example,

consider "confer" and "conference" and "prefer" and "preference." In each pair, the accent shifts from the second to the first syllable. If you add a suffix to "impulse," like say "impulsion," then the accent shifts to the second syllable. When you are learning to scan poems, it helps to use a dictionary even for simple words you think you know.

12. "Drove to this tumult in the clouds": The "Drove" is a loud variation. This line begins with a full-sounding stressed syllable, and thus it is a trochee and not an iamb. Yeats wants to emphasize the reason for the airman's risk; he is not motivated by patriotism, but rather a peculiar and personal inner drive—"a lonely impulse of delight." The trochee dramatizes the word and shows us just how helpless the airman is in the grip of this impulse. The word "tumult" is like "impulse" and "somewhere"; the accent is on the first syllable, and your dictionary will make that clear. It is an apt word here because it combines the volatility of the cloudscape with that of the airman's emotions when he is up there with them.

13. "I balanced all, brought all to mind": This line has a regular iambic beat. The only visual oddity is the word "brought"; it is a large syllable, but the **caesura** causes a pause in the line, and when we begin again we expect the same pacing, the same momentum. The repetition of the word "all" helps create this balance. Here again, the meter and sense are nicely aligned. The caesura is a fulcrum and on each side are two equal feet; the line and the idea match or balance.

14. "The years to come seemed waste of breath": This line has a regular beat; the words "waste," "breath," and "years" get obvious rhetorical accents. The word "seemed" carries some weight and is a tempting choice, but expectation and juxtaposition tend to silence it a bit. However, hearing the third foot as a spondee is certainly justifiable.

15 and 16. "A waste of breath the years behind / In balance with this life, this death": These are both regular iambic-tetrameter lines. We are back to the sense of balance here, and the repetition in the last two feet with the caesura between them demonstrates a visual as well as an auditory balance. This man is not sacrificing himself for the state. This is a coldly calculated decision he's made. The airman's life, because he lives in such a poor area of Ireland, has little chance of succeeding (no political change is likely to affect their living conditions, as he says in lines 7 and 8), so he feels that his future is as grim as his past. With nothing left to lose, he follows his instinct, his delight, regardless of the outcome.

B. **Mind**, by Richard Wilbur

1. Mind in its purest play is like some bat
2. That beats about in caverns all alone,
3. Contriving by a kind of senseless wit
4. Not to conclude against a wall of stone.
5. It has no need to falter or explore;
6. Darkly it knows what obstacles are there,
7. And so may weave and flitter, dip and soar
8. In perfect courses through the blackest air.
9. And has this simile a like perfection?
10. The mind is like a bat. Precisely. Save
11. That in the very happiest intellection
12. A graceful error may correct the cave.

This is a clever little poem that takes delight in itself and its subject. It is an **extended metaphor**: the behavior of the mind is being compared to the behavior of a bat. It expects us to know something about bat habits and abilities in order to fully appreciate the verbal play. The basic meter is iambic pentameter, and its metrical regularity is connected to its content. The mind is creating the poem and is being praised for its precision, its "perfect courses," a kind of "perfection." If the poet used a number of variations, he would lose the tidy connection between what the speaker is saying and how he is saying it. The regularity of the meter and the **end-stopped** lines make the poem's sound like the ticking of a metronome.

1. "Mind in its purest play is like some bat": The strongest syllables in this line are "mind," "pure-," "play," and "bat." The "like" gets a metrical stress, and it is clearly a stronger syllable than the ones on either side of it. It is interesting that the first foot—"Mind in"—is a metrical variation. Wilbur has used a trochee and then followed it by four iambs. The stress on this initial word of the poem suggests its importance to the whole argument. It is the subject he wishes to examine, and he seems to be saying that he wants no confusion here, because this is going to be a little lesson in precision and clarity.

2. "That beats about in caverns all alone": This line is perfectly iambic, and the main stressed syllables ("-bout," "cav-," "-lone") receive lexical stresses. There is a rhetorical stress on "beats," and the "all" gets a metrical stress.

3. "Contriving by a kind of senseless wit": Because "contriving" is a polysyllabic word, you can plot the lexical stresses by looking it up

in a dictionary. It will tell you that the accent falls on "-triv-." This line is straight iambic pentameter; the stresses are "-triv-," "by," "kind," "sense," and "wit." The "by" gets a metrical accent.

4. "Not to conclude against a wall of stone": The last four feet in this line are regular. The only question is what to do with the "not to"; the meter in the rest of the poem is so strong that the iamb comes naturally to the tongue. Yet "not" is a stronger syllable and its prominence in the line suggests it carries the accent. It makes sense that he would want to emphasize the negation; the mind is trying hard *not* to conclude against a wall. We would give "not" a rhetorical stress. The word "conclude" is a clever choice here because Wilbur utilizes several of its definitions: the end of something, the consequence of one's decision-making process, a resolution. So it is both an operation of the mind and something literal the bat might do—end its life by hitting a wall. The wall, then, has metaphoric as well as literal implications.

5. "It has no need to falter or explore": The line has a number of weak syllables, but three strong ones stand out: "need," "falt-," and "-plore." If we mark those and remember what the base meter is, then the others should be clear. The "has" gets a metrical stress. The "or" in the fourth foot is weak, but it is surrounded by weak syllables, and the iambic rhythm encourages a metrical stress here too.

6. "Darkly it knows what obstacles are there": This is an echo of line 1. "Dark-" and "knows" get rhetorical stresses. The lexical stress in "obstacles" is on the first syllable; there is a metrical stress on "-cles."

7. "And so may weave and flitter, dip and soar": The last four feet fall into a strong iambic pattern. Rhetorical considerations suggest a slight pause on "so"; it marks causation, and we tend to slightly emphasize our shifts in logic so that our listeners will keep following along.

8. "In perfect courses through the blackest air": Perhaps the only problem in scanning this line may occur if "perfect" is mispronounced; it is another of the words that change when a suffix is added, which creates a little confusion. In "perfect" the accent is on "per-," but in "perfection" the accent is on "-fec-." The word "courses" is as clever as "conclude" was above. It can mean a random trajectory or progress, deliberate tracks or plotted paths, movement in time (in the course of a year), one serving in a large meal, etc. Wilbur uses several of these definitions simultaneously.

9. "And has this simile a like perfection?" This line has five iambs, but there is an unaccented syllable left over at the end. Remember that

when a falling rhyme is used, this often happens and does not affect the scansion or the number of feet. Only a stress can produce another foot.

10. "The mind is like a bat. Precisely. Save": This line has a very regular iambic beat. Two caesuras enclose "precisely," and slow the reader down. They smugly and deliciously invite us to enjoy the precision, the mind at its clever play.

11. "That in the very happiest intellection": Each line is scanned separately, even after an enjambed ending like "Save" in line ten. This line is also in iambic pentameter, but "happiest" can be seen as either two syllables or three; if you insist on three, then there is an anapest in the fourth foot. There is no reason to put one here, and Wilbur is probably eliding (see **elision**) the syllables. The falling rhyme again produces an extra syllable at the end of this line, which is of no consequence. The initial foot is similar to that of the fourth line; if you inverted the words the meter would remain the same (not to/to not). Expectation forces the pause on the second syllable regardless of which word occupies that position.

12. "A graceful error may correct the cave": One of the many advantages of plotting the meter is understanding how the poet might be pronouncing his or her words. This line is again straight iambic pentameter, but the word "error" in common speech often gets slurred into one syllable probably because "err" is also a word. Wilbur definitely pronounces the second syllable. There isn't a reason to use a spondee here; in fact a spondee would really muddy the line as well as the ending of the poem; it would contradict all the precision he has worked so hard to maintain.

Wilbur's delight in the mind and what it can do is obvious throughout the poem; a captious critic might even call it smug. Yet the tone is so lighthearted and playful that only a very ill-humored reader could dismiss it. Furthermore, Wilbur deals with an old intellectual question, one that Keats addressed in his "Ode to a Nightingale": how our minds differ from those of other sentient beings. Keats thought our self-consciousness was something of a curse ("to think is to be full of sorrow") and wished he was more birdlike and ecstatic rather than overly reflective. Wilbur suggests that human beings have the ability to "correct the cave." We can examine and change what may have initially seemed to contain our thinking, what created boundaries. This is a happy "intellection" when it occurs—and somewhat rare—but it can occur. His choice of "intellection" is curious. It is something of a relic from Middle English when our language was more Latinized, and is not used in speech anymore. Perhaps Wilbur implies that correcting the cave can only occur through deep reflection that understands historical and intellectual influences. He manages to make this statement gracefully and subtly—he dips and soars—like a bat using its sonar to weave a perfect course through the blackest air.

    C. **Once by the Pacific**, by Robert Frost

1. The shattered water made a misty din,
2. Great waves looked over others coming in,
3. And thought of doing something to the shore
4. That water never did to land before.
5. The clouds were low and hairy in the skies
6. Like locks blown forward in the gleam of eyes.
7. You could not tell, and yet it looked as if
8. The shore was lucky in being backed by cliff,
9. The cliff in being backed by continent;
10. It looked as if a night of dark intent
11. Was coming, and not only a night, an age.
12. Someone had better be prepared for rage.
13. There would be more than ocean water broken
14. Before God's last *Put out the Light* was spoken.

1. "The shattered water made a misty din": This line is regular iambic pentameter, and its syllables and auditory effects are nicely balanced. The "-er" in "shattered" and that in "water" are snugly parallel, and the "t" in "misty" and the "d" in "din" echo each other.

2. "Great waves looked over others coming in": This line is more difficult. The first four syllables are very strong, and one can hear the line as beginning with two spondees and ending with three iambs. It is possible to hear the second foot as an iamb, but "looked" is a strong syllable. If we listen closely, we can hear the syllables of the first two feet bunch and contend with each other. They make a "misty din."

3. "And thought of doing something to the shore": This line is in regular iambs; the only difficulty might be "something," whose two syllables are well balanced. The preposition "to" is a weak syllable, but expectation and juxtaposition make this weakling stand up a little taller; it gets a metrical stress.

4 and 5. "That water never did to land before. / The clouds were

low and hairy in the skies": These two lines are regular iambic pentameter; a preposition like "in" often gets a metrical stress when it lies between two smaller syllables.

6. "Like locks blown forward in the gleam of eyes": This line is similar to line 2. You can hear the first two feet as spondees, and the blurring of stresses is similar to the **image** the poet is creating—the wind-tousled hair blurs the vision. It is possible to scan the first foot as an iamb because "like" is not as strong as "lock," and the regularity of the preceding lines might sweep us into iambs, but certainly the second foot is a spondee. "Blown" gets a rhetorical stress and "for-" gets a lexical one.

7. "You could not tell, and yet it looked as if": Regular iambic pentameter.

8. "The shore was lucky in being backed by cliff": The first two feet are iambs, but then we run into a wrinkle. The "in" is not followed by a weak syllable as it was in line five; the "be-" must get a stress. Frost has merely substituted an anapest for the third iamb. There isn't a meaningful explanation for this—and we need not always try to imagine one. The line retains its musicality, regardless.

9 and 10. "The cliff in being backed by continent; / It looked as if a night of dark intent": this is regular iambic pentameter.

11. "Was coming, and not only a night, an age": We may have some disagreement on this line, primarily because the syllables are so short and colloquial. The first foot is clearly an iamb, but then we have three short syllables in a row. Does the second stress fall on "and" or "not"? "And" is always a weak syllable, but juxtaposition will occasionally force it into a metrical stress. Content or rhetorical importance is another consideration. When reading this line, we emphasize the "not only" because we are marking a condition beyond the expected—not just a night, an age. It is possible to hear the line as containing an iamb, followed by an anapest, a trochee, an iamb, and another iamb. We could also see the second and third foot as a **super-iamb** (see page 10): iamb, pyrrhic, spondee, anapest, iamb. But the sound is the same.

12. "Someone had better be prepared for rage": Again, we have the problem of how to hear a word like "somebody" or "someone," but after a quick dictionary check, we know that the line is scanned with an initial trochee followed by iambs. That accent on "some" increases the sense of threat; it is rather accusatory. Someone had better listen, namely the reader.

13. "There would be more than ocean water broken": This line is soft and colloquial too, but the regular iambic pattern emerges with an extra falling syllable in the rhyme word.

14. "Before God's last *Put out the Light* was spoken": The difficulty with this line centers on the three middle feet. The line clearly begins with an iamb. The next four syllables are similar in length and duration. Expectation and a slight rise in emphasis make the line regularly iambic with the extra unstressed syllable in the rhyme word. It is also possible to hear it as iamb, spondee, spondee, iamb, iamb, with an extra unstressed syllable at the end.

D. **Nothing Gold Can Stay**, by Robert Frost

1. Nature's first green is gold,
2. Her hardest hue to hold.
3. Her early leaf's a flower;
4. But only so an hour.
5. Then leaf subsides to leaf.
6. So Eden sank to grief,
7. So dawn goes down to day.
8. Nothing gold can stay.

This poem is in iambic trimeter, but note that the form tolerates a little variation. The first and last lines begin with trochees, and the third line contains an extra falling syllable. In the first line, it is also possible to hear "first green" as a spondee, but "green" is clearly the stronger syllable of the two. The last line lacks the unaccented part of its third foot. Remember that when we speak of a poem as having a particular meter, we are referring to the dominant foot and the number of accents in a typical line.

One might ask why "flower" is two syllables and its rhyme word "hour" is only one. They sound similar, but "hour" has a diphthong—a speech sound where one vowel moves into another (like the "oy" in "boy"), while "flower" has two distinct syllables. The poem is scanned as follows:

$$\grave{\ } \ \breve{\ } \ | \ \breve{\ } \quad \grave{\ } \ | \breve{\ } \ \grave{\ } \quad \text{or}$$
$$\grave{\ } \ \breve{\ } \ | \ \grave{\ } \quad \grave{\ } \ | \breve{\ } \ \grave{\ }$$

Nature's first green is gold,

$$\breve{\ } \quad \grave{\ } \ | \ \breve{\ } \quad \grave{\ } \ | \breve{\ } \ \grave{\ }$$

Her hardest hue to hold.

˘　`　|　˘　`　|˘　`　|　˘
Her early leaf's a flower;

˘　`　|˘　`　|˘　`
But only so an hour,

˘　`　|　˘　`　|　˘　`
Then leaf subsides to leaf,

˘　`|　˘　`　|　˘　`
So Eden sank to grief,

˘　`　|　˘　`　|　˘　`
So dawn goes down to day.

`　|　˘　`　|　˘　`
Nothing gold can stay.

Now that you are getting good at this, we decided to challenge you with a difficult poem. You might try it one stanza at a time. Note the number of super-iambs we've included here; there are other ways to arrange the feet.

E. **Adam's Curse**, by W. B. Yeats

We sat together at one summer's end,
That beautiful mild woman, your close friend,
And you and I, and talked of poetry.
I said, "A line will take us hours maybe;
Yet if it does not seem a moment's thought,
Our stitching and unstitching has been naught.
Better go down upon your marrow-bones
And scrub a kitchen pavement, or break stones
Like an old pauper, in all kinds of weather;
For to articulate sweet sounds together
Is to work harder than all these, and yet
Be thought an idler by the noisy set
Of bankers, schoolmasters, and clergymen
The martyrs call the world."

                          And thereupon
That beautiful mild woman for whose sake
There's many a one shall find out all heartache
On finding that her voice is sweet and low
Replied, "To be born woman is to know—
Although they do not talk of it at school—
That we must labour to be beautiful."

I said "It's certain there is no fine thing
Since Adam's fall but needs much labouring.
There have been lovers who thought love should be
So much compounded of high courtesy
That they would sigh and quote with learned looks
Precedents out of beautiful old books;
Yet it seems an idle trade enough."
We sat grown quiet at the name of love.
We saw the last embers of daylight die,
And in the trembling blue-green of the sky
A moon, worn as if it had been a shell
Washed by time's waters as they rose and fell
About the stars and broke in days and years.
I had a thought for no one's but your ears:
That you were beautiful, and that I strove
To love you in the old high way of love;
That it had all seemed happy, and yet we'd grown
As weary-hearted as that hollow moon.

     ˘   ` | ˘ ` | ˘ ` | `   ` | ˘  `

1. We sat together at one summer's end,

     ˘   ` | ˘ ` | `  ` | ˘ ` | `   `

2. That beautiful mild woman, your close friend,

     ˘   ` | ˘ `| ˘ `  |˘ `|˘ `

3. And you and I, and talked of poetry.

     ˘` | ˘  ` | ˘ ` |˘  ` | ` ˘

4. I said, "A line will take us hours maybe;

     `  ˘|˘  ` | `  ` |˘ ` |˘    `   or
     `  ˘|˘  ` | ˘ ` |˘  ` |˘   `

5. Yet if it does not seem a moment's thought,

     ˘   ` | ˘  ` | ˘ ` |˘   ` | ˘ `

6. Our stitching and unstitching has been naught.

     `  ˘| ` `  | ˘ ` | ˘ ` |˘    `

7. Better go down upon your marrow-bones

     ˘   ` |˘ ` |˘ ` | ˘  ˘ | `   `

8. And scrub a kitchen pavement, or break stones

     ˘ ˘ | `   ` | ˘ `|` ` | ˘  ` | ˘

9. Like an old pauper, in all kinds of weather;

˘ ˘|˘˘|˘ ` | `   ` | ˘ `| ˘
10. For to articulate sweet sounds together

˘ ˘ | `     ` | ˘   `| ` ` | ˘  `
11. Is to work harder than all these, and yet

˘ `    | ˘  `|˘ `| ˘  `|˘ `
12. Be thought an idler by the noisy set

˘ ` |˘      ` | ` ˘  | ˘     `| ˘ `
13. Of bankers, schoolmasters, and clergymen

˘   ` | ˘ ` | ˘   ` |
14. The martyrs call the world."

˘   `  |˘ `
And thereupon

˘   ` | ˘`| `     `| ˘ ` | ˘     `
15. That beautiful mild woman for whose sake

˘   ` | ˘ ˘ ` | ˘   `  | ` `| `   `
16. There's many a one shall find out all heartache

˘ ` | ˘   ` | ˘   ` |˘   ` | ˘   `
17. On finding that her voice is sweet and low

˘ `   | ˘ ˘ | `   `| ˘  `|˘   `
18. Replied, "To be born woman is to know—

˘ `  | ˘   `| `   ` | ˘˘|˘ `
19. Although they do not talk of it at school—

˘ ` | ˘   ` | ˘ ` | ˘   ` |˘`
20. That we must labour to be beautiful."

˘ `| ˘  `| ˘   `  | ˘ `| `   `
21. I said "It's certain there is no fine thing

˘ `| ˘    `| ˘ ` | ˘  `| ˘`   `
22. Since Adam's fall but needs much labouring.

˘ ` | ˘  `|˘   ` | `   ` | ˘   `
23. There have been lovers who thought love should be

`  ` | ˘ ` | ˘ `| `    ` | ˘ `   or

˘ ` | ˘  ` | ˘ `| `   ` | ˘ `
24. So much compounded of high courtesy

˘   ˋ | ˘   ˋ | ˘   ˋ | ˘   ˋ | ˘   ˋ
25. That they would sigh and quote with learned looks

ˋ   ˘| ˘   ˋ |˘   ˋ |˘ˋ |ˋ   ˋ
26. Precedents out of beautiful old books;

ˋ | ˘   ˋ |˘ ˋ |˘   ˋ |˘   ˋ
27. Yet it seems an idle trade enough."

˘ ˋ | ˋ   ˋ|˘ ˋ|˘   ˋ | ˘ ˋ
28. We sat grown quiet at the name of love

˘   ˋ |˘   ˋ |˘   ˋ |˘ ˋ | ˘   ˋ   or
˘   ˋ |˘   ˋ |ˋ   ˘ |˘ˋ |ˋ   ˋ
29. We saw the last embers of daylight die,

ˋ   ˘|˘ ˋ | ˘   ˋ | ˋ   ˘ |˘ ˋ
30. And in the trembling blue-green of the sky

˘   ˋ | ˋ   ˘ |ˋ ˘| ˘   ˋ |˘ ˋ
31. A moon, worn as if it had been a shell

ˋ   ˘ | ˋ   ˋ|˘   ˋ | ˘   ˋ | ˘ ˋ
32. Washed by time's waters as they rose and fell

˘ ˋ |˘   ˋ | ˘   ˋ |˘   ˋ | ˘ ˋ
33. About the stars and broke in days and years.

ˋ ˘ |˘   ˋ | ˘ ˋ| ˘   ˋ | ˘   ˋ   or
˘ ˋ |˘   ˋ | ˘ ˋ| ˘   ˋ |ˋ   ˋ
34. I had a thought for no one's but your ears:

˘   ˋ | ˘   ˋ |˘ˋ |˘   ˘ |ˋ ˋ
35. That you were beautiful, and that I strove

˘ ˋ | ˘   ˋ|˘ ˋ| ˋ   ˋ |˘ ˋ
36. To love you in the old high way of love;

˘   ˋ|˘   ˋ| ˘   ˋ|˘ ˘   ˋ|˘   ˋ   or
ˋ   ˘|˘   ˋ| ˘   ˋ|˘ ˘   ˋ|˘   ˋ
37. That it had all seemed happy, and yet we'd grown

˘   ˋ |˘   ˋ|˘ ˋ|˘   ˋ|˘   ˋ   or
˘   ˋ |˘   ˋ|˘ ˘   ˋ|ˋ   ˘ | ˋ
38. As weary-hearted as that hollow moon.

9 Heartbeat and Diurnal Cycles

Many people have theorized about why meter pleases in some very basic way. It takes only a little observation to know that children, with no understanding of theory or metrics, will not only start to make up rhymes, but will also employ metrical schemes; they will recognize when a meter locks in, and they are disturbed when it does not. Some writers have claimed that the pulse we hear in metrical poetry ultimately derives from the heartbeat, and there is some relation between scansion marks in a poem and the EKG printout. We feel and hear the heartbeat, and we're steadied by it. If that regular heartbeat flutters or skips, we're either in love or in deep trouble. That constant thumping does seem very close to the metrical beat, and our awareness of it is similarly unconscious. If we needed more examples of regularity, it wouldn't take long to find them: the diurnal cycle, the monthly cycle, the rotation of the seasons. But it's the shorter cycles that seem the most obvious source; the others merely point out that we are aware of and take a certain comfort in any recurrences short enough to catch our attention.

In addition to the regular thumping of our heartbeats, there is respiration. Modern poets, looking to justify a less-regular prosody, have talked about the line as a breath unit. The limitations that the breath places on possible line lengths are akin to the regularity of the heartbeat. We can only inhale or exhale so long, and we can only wait for the next breath so long.

Still, traditional meter is concerned with more fixed regularities. In music, composers not only decide on a time signature, they often measure how many beats there are per minute. Poetry is less exact in its time signatures, but its meters can be just as precise.

Another way to put this is that regular recurring accent starts up a pattern of expectation. We know what to expect, and we begin to depend on it. This is similar to the way our minds code other information. For example, once you learn the number of steps you have to climb (assuming it's a relatively small number) from the street to your house, you store that information and can almost read a book while walking up them. You expect the landing at a certain point. If a step is deleted, you can get in trouble. Your body is ready to climb another step, so you stumble. Similarly, if you tap your foot in time with music, you know when the musicians miss a beat. If the group is unable to keep a steady pace, the music becomes undanceable. However, the expectation pattern also allows for surprises. Syncopation is a surprise—a misplacement of the beat—which had better return to the basic pattern, or it's no longer syncopation but arrhythmia. Musicians, like poets, keep reinforcing the expectation pattern, so that occasionally they can depart from it for emphasis.

10 Meter, Rhythm, and Degrees of Stress

Although we have ignored the duration of a syllable in favor of a simple binary system of stressed or unstressed syllables, duration does have a role in the rhythm of a line. T. S. Omond, in his book called *English Metrists*, wrote that one of the basic components in metered lines of poetry is "the opposition between syllabic and temporal structure" (268). The rhythmic effects of a line are as much a product of the arrangement of stresses as the durational interplay of the syllables themselves. The scansion system we have been using emphasizes what might be called the "ground beat" in meter. We try to hear the poem's pulse, its steady rhythm or the rhythm that's implied. This is what the bass drum plays in the band, the beat that keeps everyone together; it is what the soloist always returns to. In order to find this implied regularity, we have been treating all accents similarly. For purposes of determining base meter, this is the best strategy to use. We don't want to make it too complex initially; our main purpose is to find the central pulse of the line and then to examine the variations.

Many linguists and prosodists speak of degrees of stress. An example cited by Alex Preminger and T. V. F. Brogan in *The New Princeton Encyclopedia of Poetry and Poetics* is from Andrew Marvell's "The Garden":

      3 4   2   1   3 4   2   1
      To a green thought in a green shade. (1993, 1008)

The numbers correspond to levels of stress in the line (in this case, 4 is the least and 1 is the most). The words "thought" and "shade" have the most stress, while "green" is close but has slightly less. The prepositions "to" and "in" have more weight than the article "a." It is perhaps helpful to think of stress in these terms because we feel better if we miss by a mere degree than if we miss outright. But it is not helpful in any practical way; hearing these different levels won't allow us to plot the scansion of a line more "accurately."

It is easier to think of stress in binary terms: a syllable is either accented or it isn't. To our ears, the Marvell line can be read so that "green" is given a rhetorical stress equal to "thought" or "shade," depending on how one reads the line. We hear the line as two super-iambs, and we don't mark distinctions between qualities of stress.

Differences of opinion among prosodists about the way a particular line is scanned generally stem from some private notion of degrees of stress. For example, Paul Fussell, in *Poetic Meter and Poetic Form*, scans a Frost line this way:

˘　˘　ˋ　　˘　˘　ˋ　　˘　˘　ˋ

as I came to the edge of the wood,

ˋ　　˘　˘　　ˋ

Thrush music—Hark! (1979, 34)

Fussell ignores the lexical stress on "music," but we can lean our ears his way and hear it as he does. This is not, though, the only way to hear the line. Whether we hear a spondee in the first foot of the second line or a reversed foot followed by an iamb all depends on what's "'in' the reader's mind and musculature," as Fussell himself points out (4). The reader who hears a spondee in "Thrush music" exalts more in the apprehension of the thrush's music than in the thrush; the reader who hears the foot as a trochee emphasizes the thrush more than the music—he's more of a bird-watcher than a musician. One reading isn't inherently better or more correct than the other, and as Fussell has also pointed out, "The goal of what we are doing is enjoyment: an excessive refinement of terms and categories may impress others, but it will probably not help us very much to appreciate English poetic rhythms" (21). The argument holds for those who dogmatically insist on one way of scanning a line when another way may be just as plausible: enjoyment is the goal, not correctness.

However, two lines that are both in perfect iambic pentameter can have very different sounds. In fact, a good poet may not want to vary the meter much, but still want variety in the lines. How is this achieved? The simple answer is by varying the top beat while keeping the bottom beat steady. In practice, that means the poet has three or four relatively strong beats (like "green" and "shade") but keeps the relatively weak beats to one or two. In other words, there are one or two metrical accents in a line. This is seen most easily in the opening two stanzas of Marvell's "The Definition of Love:"

1. My Love is of a birth as rare
2. As 'tis, for object, strange and high;
3. It was begotten by Despair
4. Upon Impossibility.

5. Magnanimous Despair alone
6. Could show me so divine a thing,

7. Where feeble Hope could ne'er have flown
8. But vainly flapped its tinsel wing.

This is very regular iambic tetrameter. A quick analysis shows that the principal accents in line 1 are "Love," "birth," and "rare," with a metrical accent on "of." Line 2 is similarly easy to scan. The two-syllable word "object" is accented on the first syllable. The remaining accents are on "'tis," "strange," and "high." The remaining lines are also fairly easy to hear; the most difficult is, perhaps, line 4, where the main accent is on the syllable "pos-" and secondary accents are on "bil-" and "-ty."

If each of the lines has eight syllables and starts with an unaccented syllable, and the accents are on alternating syllables, then why does the rhythm seem so varied? The heavy accents are quite heavy and the light accents are quite light. The regular beat is there, but other rhythms play on top. If you pay attention to the heavy accents generated by primary accents in polysyllabic words and by rhetorical accents on the one-syllable words, you find that the rhythm of the lines is something like this:

1. ˘ ˋ ˘ ˘ ˋ ˘ ˘ ˋ
2. ˘ ˋ ˘ ˋ ˘ ˋ ˘ ˋ
3. ˘ ˘ ˘ ˘ ˋ ˘ ˘ ˋ
4. ˘ ˋ ˘ ˋ ˘ ˘ ˘
5. ˘ ˋ ˘ ˘ ˋ ˘ ˘ ˋ
6. ˘ ˋ ˘ ˘ ˘ ˋ ˘ ˋ
7. ˘ ˋ ˘ ˋ ˘ ˋ ˘ ˋ
8. ˘ ˋ ˘ ˋ ˘ ˋ ˘ ˋ

In line 1, we have a rhythm of three strong accents against five weaker syllables. And in line 4, two strong against five weak ones. Even line 7, which we have shown as four against four, could be seen as three against five with the "ne'er" as being more lightly accented.

This is a rather subtle concept. The common way of achieving variety is by substitution: a metrical foot that deviates from the one used as the prevailing meter of the poem. If the meter is iambic, then a spondee, trochee, anapest, or dactyl substituted for one of the iambs would be a substitution or variation. Substituting a spondee for an iamb causes the least turmoil. Our expectation of pattern is fulfilled: we get the accent where we expect it. But we get another one as well. A more violent substitution in an iambic meter is a trochee, which reverses the order of the accented and unaccented syllables while leaving the number of syllables unchanged. A trochee in an iambic poem is called a *re-*

versed foot, for obvious reasons. Similarly, an iamb in a trochaic meter, or a dactyl in an anapestic meter, or an anapest in a dactylic meter would also be a reversed foot. If you replace an iamb with an anapest, you get another kind of substitution. The foot is one syllable longer, but it does end with an accent, as we would expect.

There is another way of producing a variation in the rhythm of a line. If you are writing in iambic meter and use one- and two-syllable words and arrange them so that the iambs always appear at the end of the two-syllable words or on an accented one-syllable word, the effect will be a very pronounced meter. Marvell's line 6 is like this: "could show me so divine a thing." The accents on one-syllable words like "show," "so," and "thing," and the accent on the second syllable of "divine," create a very strong rhythm. Poems that stay too close to this pattern sound predictable, like clocks ticking away. If the metrical boundaries (the ends of feet) appear in the middle of words, it is harder to hear the feet as feet, and the meter seems smoother, less persistent. In the first line of the Marvell poem, the metrical boundaries coincide perfectly with the word boundaries; in the second line, they do not, nor do they coincide in lines 3, 4, 5, 7, or 8.

11 Some Fine Points

The Pyrrhic Foot

A syllable is stressed if it is accented more strongly than its neighbors. For example, if the word is long enough, the dictionary will indicate secondary stress as well as primary stress. No distinction is made between degrees among the secondary stresses. Fussell has isolated four "phonetic qualities" of words: pitch, loudness, length, and timbre ("fuzziness, hoarseness, sharpness," etc.), but he goes on to say how difficult it is to isolate qualities of the accented syllable (1979, 9). Distinction in duration and harshness are important in what we have called the top and bottom beat of a line, but not the way we scan it. Furthermore, when polysyllabic words are pronounced the way we would say them, stress occurs at regular intervals; there are few words in English that have three unaccented syllables in a row. And the examples we have discovered are created by adding suffixes like -able or -ly to an already prefixed or suffixed word like "un-no-tice-a-ble" or "un-men-tion-a-ble." We would argue that the "-ble" would probably be stressed in a metrical environment. In fact, if we add another suffix to this already overloaded word and get "un-men-tion-a-bil-it-y," we notice that it is the "-bil-" that gets the secondary stress. A line of metrical poetry reacts similarly, and generally a preposition or suffix between two unstressed syllables gets a metrical stress. Let's consider a few examples of the pyrrhic foot chosen by prosodists, who tend to find them more frequently than we do.

In his book *Western Wind*, John Frederick Nims uses the following two examples:

ˇ ˋ | ˇ ˇ | ˇ ˋ | ˇ ˇ | ˇ ˋ

Advantage on the kingdom of the shore
  (William Shakespeare; 1974, 233)

ˇ ˋ | ˇ ˋ | ˇ ˋ | ˇ ˇ | ˋ ˋ

I feel the ladder sway as the boughs bend. (Robert Frost; 234)

Clement Wood, in his *Poets' Handbook,* also chose a line from Shakespeare to illustrate a pyrrhic:

ˇ ˋ | ˇ ˋ | ˇ ˇ | ˇ ˋ | ˇ ˋ | ˇ

The slings and arrows of outrageous fortune (1940, 145)

Derek Attridge, in *The Rhythms of English Poetry*, uses the following quotation from Wordsworth:

    ˇ ˋ | ˇ ˋ| ˇ ˇ | ˇ ˋ

Behold her, single in the field. (1982, 7)

Fussell finds two pyrrhics in the following lines by Yeats:

    ˇ ˋ |ˇ ˋ |ˇ ˇ |ˇ ˋ |ˇ ˋ

An aged man is but a paltry thing,

    ˇ ˋ | ˇ ˋ | ˇ ˇ |ˇ ˋ | ˇ ˋ

A tattered coat upon a stick, unless (33)

Our differences with these critics center on what we have called the metrical stress. In Nims's first example, the "on" in the second foot gets a stress—albeit a weak one. Similarly, in Wood's quotation, "of" in the third foot gets a stress. It is difficult to say these lines without hearing a slight rise in the rhythm; certainly, in the first instance, the "on" is pronounced with more stress than "-tage" or "the." We feel the same way about the "in" of the third foot in Attridge's quotation. We do agree that the pyrrhic is found in the Frost line, but it appears at the end of the line in what we have called a "super-iamb." Attridge calls this combination of two unstressed syllables followed by two stressed "one of the commonest variations in duple verse" (24); by "duple" he means feet with two syllables, namely iambic and trochaic meters. Most frequently, the super-iamb occurs at the end or the beginning of the line; however, occasionally, it can be found in the middle, as in this line from one of Keats's sonnets, called "When I Have Fears":

    ˋ ˇ | ˋ ˋ | ˇ ˇ | ˋ ˋ |ˇ ˋ

Hold like rich garners the full-ripen'd grain.

In the Fussell example from Yeats, the "but" in the first line makes a significant logical and tonal contribution to the meaning and thus has rhetorical import; it's also in the right position to receive a stress. Fussell says, "These substitutions serve both to relieve the metrical monotony of the long-continued, unvaried iambic pentameter and to allow the rhythmical structure to 'give' and shape itself according to the rhetorical pressures of the statement. And the rhythmical shaping is noticeable only because it takes place against the background of the 'silent' metrical continuum" (33). Fussell is speaking in general terms, and we agree with his observation. The Yeats poem in question, however, has no "metrical monotony" to relieve. The lines Fussell quotes from "Sailing to Byzantium" are at the beginning of the second stanza. In the first stanza, four of the eight lines have metrical variations, including lines 7 and 8—the two preceding the lines he quotes. Therefore, the iambic meter in Yeats's poem is neither "long-continued" nor "unvaried." Yeats is most likely putting a stress on "but," as most readers will. The identification of a pyrrhic in the second line, though, is justifiable; there is a lexical stress on "-on," but neither syllable has much weight or meaning in this line. Yeats is varying the top and bottom beat that we described in Chapter 10, "Meter, Rhythm, and Degrees of Stress." Whether we want to call the third foot a pyrrhic or an iamb with a very weak stress is simply a matter of taste.

We find that identifying metrical accents leads to more accurate descriptions of how the line is actually read. The pyrrhic foot was always an exception. The most basic definition of meter is "regularly recurring stress," and the pyrrhic foot has no stress.

Variant Pronunciations

How do you pronounce a word that may have been pronounced differently at the time the poem was written? What do you do with words pronounced differently in the United States and England—and suppose you don't know the nationality of the author? And suppose you do? What about words that seem to have different syllable counts depending on your pronunciation scheme? The answer is the same in all cases: you have a choice. You can try to find out how the author pronounced the word and then use that pronunciation for your work, or you can indicate that you are using present-day American pronunciation. Classical music offers examples of a similar choice. Pieces written for the harpsichord were later (and still are) often played on the piano, a very different-sounding and more recently developed instrument. Yet today, there has been a growing interest in "period" performances, performances on instruments the composer knew and wrote for—a desire to hear what the composer heard. In a similar way, we have two choices about how to perform a poem.

If you know which words have changed and you are trying to indicate how the line was read, you can use your historical knowledge. For example, in eighteenth-century England, "tea" was pronounced as in French, "thé" (tay). In British English, "laboratory" is pronounced with the accent on the second syllable, "la-bór-a-tree." In American English, it's pronounced with the accent on the first syllable, "láb-ra-tor-ee." It is also possible that you may be more interested in how a poem sounds in contemporary American English, the language you're used to. This may make the poem seem more contemporary. After all, why pretend to speak the poem in a variation of English you don't use or know very well? All are acceptable solutions. When in doubt, simply explain which you have chosen.

The Special Case of "-ed"

Historically, there is something of a split decision about what to do with accent marks and apostrophes. For example, what do we do with words in poems with accent marks like "piléd" and those with apostrophes like "work'd"? The accent and apostrophe are editorial techniques (and old spelling conventions) used to indicate whether "-ed" is a syllable or is simply pronounced "d." Notice that the accent in "piléd" is still on the first syllable; the accent mark on the "ed" is just telling us that the "ed" is to be pronounced as a separate syllable.

When spelling was becoming standardized, two different methods were used to show how a final "-ed" was pronounced. The past tense marker "-ed" was often pronounced as an extra syllable. What we now pronounce as "workt" used to be "work+ed" or "workéd." Consider, for example, this line from a sonnet by Keats: "that deep-brow'd Homer ruled as his demesne." To make sure we don't pronounce "brow'd" as two syllables, he puts in the apostrophe. Since we pronounce "browed" as one syllable already, it seems extraneous to us. But some words kept their original pronunciation—like "offended" ("o-fend-did"). For a while words may have had two pronunciations and, to help indicate which was intended, two printing conventions were devised. If "ed" was not pronounced, the printer replaced it with an apostrophe; so if you saw "ed," you pronounced it as a syllable. Other printers wanted to indicate that "ed" was pronounced by accenting the "e," as in "weddéd." If there were no accent, you didn't pronounce it as a separate syllable. And, of course, some combined both techniques and used apostrophes and accents. You can see the two conventions at work in the following lines, which are also from Keats:

> If by dull rhymes our English must be chain'd
>   And, like Andromeda, the Sonnet sweet
> Fetter'd, in spite of painéd loveliness.

Here, "chain'd" is pronounced as one syllable and "fetter'd" as two. But in "painéd," Keats needed an extra syllable to make his last three feet more regular. At the beginning of the nineteenth century, metrical regularity, or a poet's "numbers" as Pope called it, was still a major criterion for judging a poet's work. If Keats had not accented the "-ed" in "pained," he would have had three metrical variations in that line instead of one.

A Note on Trisyllabic Meters

A problem with the approach we've taken is that it doesn't seem to work well in the case of anapestic meter. Too many accents show up, often in the wrong places.

From **The Destruction of Sennacherib**

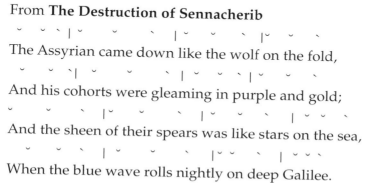

The Assyrian came down like the wolf on the fold,

And his cohorts were gleaming in purple and gold;

And the sheen of their spears was like stars on the sea,

When the blue wave rolls nightly on deep Galilee.

If you look at the first stanza of Byron's "The Destruction of Sennacherib," the problem becomes clear. The poem is in anapestic tetrameter. The second line is easy to scan—it's a perfect example of the meter, as is the third line, which is totally monosyllabic. But what of the first and last lines? The verb "came down" is phrasal, so it makes sense to accent "down." If "blue" is accented in the fourth line, as it needs to be for the meter, then how can we not accent "wave" and "rolls"? These are good questions. Questions similar to them come up at various points in the poem.

The simplest answer is that **trisyllabic** meters employ a different criterion for accent than **disyllabic** meters. That sounds like special pleading, and maybe it is, but trisyllabic meters are nowhere near as common in English as disyllabic meters, and do have special qualities. The main thing that keeps a metrical rhythm going is "regular recurring stress." Regularity is what leads to predictability and that leads to anticipation. Satisfy the anticipation for accents and you will produce a metrical line. To say that another way, if you find the accents occurring at a regular interval in the places they should be, then the effect is metrical. What we want to suggest is that in trisyllabic meters, a syllable is accented if it's hit hard and only if it's hit hard. In the fourth line of the poem, the accents are on "blue," "night," "deep," and "-lee" (the lexical demand puts the stress on "Gal-" in Galilee, but Byron is probably accenting "-lee" to make his meter come out right; we could see it as a dactylic substitution, but we suspect that Byron wishes to exhibit his skill with meter). The stresses are in the right places. We have an expectation pattern. And although "waves" and "roll" in the second foot of that line are somewhat stressed, in an anapestic poem a stressed syllable is really stressed hard. That's the difference between disyllabic and trisyllabic meters. Perhaps the wait to get to the accent—since it's a bit longer in trisyllabic than in a disyllabic poem—results in a harder hit.

Anapestic and dactylic meters thump along regularly like a tire with a bulge in it. It's hard to use them for serious subjects: they seem to be having too much fun on their own. At times even two-syllable words may be treated as if both syllables are unaccented. And an adjective—like "blue"—can be more heavily stressed than the noun it modifies—"wave"—or even the verb—"rolls"—that follows; both are submerged by expectation. To hit the stress, you have to whack the syllable; gentle taps, which count in iambic poems, are too subtle for trisyllabic waters. It is this steady thumping that makes this meter too raucous for thoughtful poems. We either get intentional humor, as in some of Robert Service poems like "The Cremation of Sam McGee," or unintentional humor, in what were supposed to be serious poems.

A Note on Sapphics

In *A Handbook to Literature*, C. Hugh Holman and William Harmon define *sapphics* as a Greek stanza form of three lines, each consisting of a trochee, a spondee, a dactyl, a trochee, and a trochee, followed by a fourth line consisting of a dactyl and a trochee. This is the meter the Greek poet Sappho used for her poems in the sixth century BCE. Greek meter is **quantitative**, which means that in Greek metrics, *iamb* refers to a short syllable, (one with a short vowel), followed by a long syllable, (one with a long vowel). But **iamb** in English refers to any unstressed syllable followed by a stressed one.

This has led to considerable confusion. One source of the confusion has been the Greek convention for marking feet. In Greek meter one scans an iamb as (˘¯) rather than (˘`) i.e., short-long rather than unstress-stress. But the more serious confusion has to do with the enormous difference between our abilities to recognize quantity and accent in English. Although a few poets have tried to write Greek quantitative verse in English, the results have been mixed at best. **Accent** is not only native to English concepts of rhythm, it is also much more prominent. The recurrence of long syllables—not just a repeated long "a" as in "say," but any recurring combination of long "a" and "e" or "o" sounds—is generally not discernible to an ear trained in English.

Nonetheless, there have been two methods of writing sapphics. Thomas Campion and Algernon Charles Swinburne attempted the quantitative sort, but unsuccessfully. Hardy is among those who attempted the second method (in the traditional English sense of stress). Hardy's poem "The Temporary the All" bears the subtitle "Sapphics" in parentheses. It's a good thing it does because without that help, we doubt anyone would know what to make of the meter. Perhaps in an attempt to produce a Greek flavor, Hardy has not used rhyme. We don't think it's possible to hear the meter as "sapphic," though we do hear something. A look at the first two stanzas will show what's involved.

> Change and chancefulness in my flowering youthtime,
> Set me sun by sun near to one unchosen;
> Wrought us fellowlike, and despite divergence,
>   Fused us in friendship.

> 'Cherish him can I while the true one forthcome—
> Come the rich fulfiller of my prevision;
> Life is roomy yet, and the odds unbounded.'
>   So self-communed I.

The prominent use of a stress on the first syllable of each line sets the meter of the poem off from iambic poetry. It probably prepares us for trochaic meter—dactylic meter is very rare. But we can also hear many places where we seem to have some trisyllabic feet. More than that is beyond our ears. Since Hardy has told us how he wants the poem read, we can mark it according to the sapphic requirements and look at what this reveals.

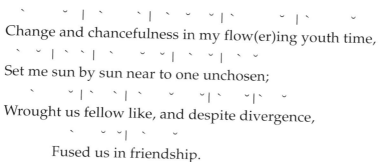

`  ˇ  |  `   `  |`   ˇ   ˇ | `    ˇ  |  `   ˇ

'Cherish him can I while the true one forth come—

`     ˇ  |  `   `  |` ˇ ˇ | `    ˇ  |`   ˇ

Come the rich fulfiller of my prevision;

`   ˇ|  `   `  |  `   ˇ   ˇ | `    ˇ  |    `   ˇ

Life is roomy yet, and the odds unbounded.'

`    ˇ    ˇ  |  `   ˇ

So self-communed I.

Hardy manages the feet of the short last line of the first stanza success-fully. In the short line of the second stanza we hear an accent on the second syllable, "self." The biggest problem he has is getting three accents in a row in the longer lines. But his spondees are rarely true spondees: "chanceful," "sun by," and "roomy" are not spondees. The weak syllables of the dactyl and the two trochees work well, however.

We read Hardy's poem in stanzas of three eleven-syllable lines (we assume he wants "flowering" pronounced "flow'ring") with one five-syllable line. The general pulse of the poem is dactylic. But there is often a disturbance in the middle of the line that throws off the rhythm. We struggle to get back to a recognizable pattern.

Hardy is generally thought of as a poet with "rough" meters. We can be grateful that he told us what meter he was aiming for, but we don't have to agree that it was successful. Yet the poem has merits despite its metrical problems.

12 More Practice with Scansion

Prescansion Exercise

We have marked the syllables in the following words as being either stressed or unstressed; if these words were in a poem, we would be marking their lexical stresses: the primary and the secondary.

1. ob-ser-va-tion

2. pan-the-on

3. par-tic-u-lar (the "-lar" might get a metrical stress in a poem)

4. de-bat-a-ble (the "-ble" might get a metrical stress in a poem)

5. di-ag-on-al (the "-al" might get a metrical stress in a poem)

6. de-vo-tion-al (the "-al" might get a metrical stress in a poem)

7. grad-u-a-tion

8. in-de-pen-dent

9. lib-er-ty (the "-ty" might get a metrical stress in a poem)

10. mod-er-ate (the verb form); the adjective form is ` ˘ ˘ ˘

The following lines are scanned for you; note that "come" in line 4 and "much" in line 5 are rhetorical stresses, as are "pure" in line 9 and "old griefs" in line 15.

1. The sea is calm tonight (Matthew Arnold, "Dover Beach")

2. The tide is full, the moon lies fair (Arnold; "lies fair" could be a spondee.)

˘ ˋ ˘ ˋ ˘ ˋ ˘ ˋ ˘ ˋ

3. its melancholy, long, withdrawing roar (Arnold)

ˋ ˘ ˘ ˋ ˘ ˋ ˘ ˘ ˋ ˋ

4. Come to the window, sweet is the night-air (Arnold)

ˋ ˘ ˘ ˋ ˘ ˘ ˋ ˋ ˘ ˋ

5. Much have I traveled in the realms of gold (John Keats, "On First Looking into Chapman's Homer"; the "in" is a metrical stress in this iambic-pentameter sonnet.)

˘ ˋ ˘ ˋ ˘ ˋ ˘ ˋ ˘ ˋ

6. And many goodly states and kingdoms seen (Keats)

˘ ˋ ˘ ˋ ˘ ˋ ˘ ˋ ˘ ˋ

7. Thy soul was like a star, and dwelt apart (William Wordsworth, "London, 1802"; it is possible to hear a spondee in the first foot, where "thy" gets a rhetorical accent.)

˘ ˋ ˘ ˋ ˘ ˋ ˘ ˋ ˘ ˋ

8. Thou hadst a voice whose sound was like the sea (Wordsworth)

ˋ ˘ ˘ ˋ ˘ ˋ ˘ ˘ ˋ ˋ

9. Pure as the naked heavens, majestic, free (Wordsworth)

˘ ˋ ˘ ˋ ˘ ˘ ˋ ˘ ˋ ˋ

10. Your door is shut against my tightened face (Claude McKay, "The White House")

˘ ˋ ˘ ˋ ˘ ˋ ˘ ˋ

11. We passed the School, where Children strove (Emily Dickinson, "Because I could not stop for Death")

˘ ˋ ˘ ˋ ˘ ˋ ˘ ˋ

12. We passed the fields of Gazing Grain (Dickinson)

˘ ˋ ˘ ˋ ˘ ˘ ˋ ˘ ˋ ˘ ˘ ˋ ˘ ˋ ˘ ˋ

13. I lean and loaf at my ease observing a spear of summer grass (Walt Whitman, "Song of Myself")

˘ ˋ ˘ ˋ ˘ ˋ ˘ ˋ ˘ ˋ

14. I love thee with the passion put to use (Elizabeth Barrett Browning, "Sonnets from the Portuguese 43"; it is possible to hear the "thee" as a rhetorical accent, although this sonnet has six lines that start this way, undermining this rhetorical effect—if it were stressed, nonetheless, then the "with" would not be stressed.)

15. in my old griefs, and with my childhood's faith (Browning; it is also possible to read the first two feet as iambs, so "my" and "griefs" are accented and "in" and "old" are not.)

Eight Poems

We have included eight more poems so that you can practice your scansion; we have included our scansion of these poems afterward with a minimal amount of commentary, and that only on the lines that seem most difficult.

A. **Blessing**, by Judith Kleck (1983)

1. Across the Strait of Juan de Fuca, northeast
2. and out of nothing, Baker stuns the thin
3. blue air. How odd the mountain first should bring
4. the art to mind: impossible to see
5. it free of Hokusai, or you, your lean
6. collages—strong, spare—where color swings
7. its object open like a door. I think
8. of loves we share: green shades, good gin, Matisse,
9. the rituals of food. Yet our separate arts
10. define our separate lives. A heron keels
11. across the Sound. We are absorbed by these
12. inventions, puzzling mountains into parts
13. until a suddenness of vision yields
14. a wholeness up: relinquished, we are blessed.

B. **Delight in Disorder**, by Robert Herrick (1648)

1. A sweet disorder in the dress
2. Kindles in clothes a wantonness.
3. A lawn about the shoulders thrown
4. Into a fine distraction;
5. An erring lace, which here and there
6. Enthralls the crimson stomacher;
7. A cuff neglectful, and thereby
8. Ribbons to flow confusedly;
9. A winning wave, deserving note,
10. In the tempestuous petticoat;
11. A careless shoestring, in whose tie
12. I see a wild civility;

13. Do more bewitch me than when art
14. Is too precise in every part.

C. **The Dance (in Breughel's)**, by William Carlos Williams (1944)

1. In Breughel's great picture, The Kermess,
2. the dancers go round, they go round and
3. around, the squeeze and the blare and the
4. tweedle of bagpipes, a bugle and fiddles
5. tipping their bellies (round as the thick-
6. sided glasses whose wash they impound)
7. their hips and their bellies off balance
8. to turn them. Kicking and rolling about
9. the Fair Grounds, swinging their butts, those
10. shanks must be sound to bear up under such
11. rollicking measures, prance as they dance
12. in Breughel's great picture, The Kermess.

D. **One Art**, by Elizabeth Bishop (1976)

1. The art of losing isn't hard to master;
2. so many things seem filled with the intent
3. to be lost that their loss is no disaster.

4. Lose something every day. Accept the fluster
5. of lost door keys, the hour badly spent.
6. The art of losing isn't hard to master.

7. Then practice losing farther, losing faster:
8. places, and names, and where it was you meant
9. to travel. None of these will bring disaster.

10. I lost my mother's watch. And look! my last, or
11. next-to-last, of three loved houses went.
12. The art of losing isn't hard to master.

13. I lost two cities, lovely ones. And, vaster,
14. some realms I owned, two rivers, a continent.
15. I miss them, but it wasn't a disaster.

16. —Even losing you (the joking voice, a gesture
17. I love) I shan't have lied. It's evident
18. the art of losing's not too hard to master
19. though it may look like (*Write* it!) like disaster.

E. **Étude**, by A. E. Stallings (2002)

1. She fingers it with something like regret,
2. Clasping at its neck, stopping a string.
3. A ghostly music scrapes beneath her ring,
4. Some measure of a song she can't forget.
5. She's half a heart to play again, and yet
6. How it reproaches—mute, abandoned thing:
7. Rote afternoons beat out in practicing
8. Dead-end arpeggios, the minuet,
9. The metronome's long finger on the sill
10. Wagging, no, no—again; the click of clocks
11. As she trudged up the scales, the little rut
12. Worn in the brain and fingertips, until
13. The hour dismissed her at the last and shut
14. The fretful instrument back in its box.

F. **After great pain, a formal feeling comes**—by Emily Dickinson (1862?)

1. After great pain, a formal feeling comes—
2. The Nerves sit ceremonious, like Tombs—
3. The stiff Heart questions was it He, that bore,
4. And Yesterday, or Centuries before?

5. The Feet, mechanical, go round—
6. Of Ground, or Air, or Ought—
7. A Wooden way
8. Regardless grown,
9. A Quartz contentment, like a stone—

10. This is the Hour of Lead—
11. Remembered, if outlived,
12. As Freezing Persons recollect the Snow—
13. First—Chill—then Stupor—then the letting go.

G. **Aunt Jennifer's Tigers**, by Adrienne Rich (1950)

1. Aunt Jennifer's tigers prance across the screen,
2. Bright topaz denizens of a world of green.
3. They do not fear the men beneath the tree;
4. They pace in sleek chivalric certainty.
5. Aunt Jennifer's fingers fluttering through her wool
6. Find even the ivory needle hard to pull.

7. The massive weight of Uncle's wedding band
8. Sits heavily upon Aunt Jennifer's hand.
9. When Aunt is dead, her terrified hands will lie
10. Still ringed by ordeals she was mastered by.
11. The tigers in the panel that she made
12. Will go on prancing, proud and unafraid.

H. **Incident**, by Countee Cullen (1925)

1. Once riding in old Baltimore
2.   Heart-filled, head-filled with glee,
3. I saw a Baltimorean
4.   Keep looking straight at me.

5. Now I was eight and very small,
6.   And he was no whit bigger,
7. And so I smiled, but he poked out
8.   His tongue, and called me "Nigger."

9. I saw the whole of Baltimore
10.   From May until December;
11. Of all the things that happened there
12.   That's all that I remember.

A. **Blessing**, by Judith Kleck (1983)

    ˘   ˋ | ˘   ˋ | ˘   ˋ | ˘ ˋ|˘   ˘   ˋ

1. Across the Strait of Juan de Fuca, northeast

    ˘   ˋ|˘   ˋ |˘   ˋ|˘   ˋ | ˘   ˋ

2. and out of nothing, Baker stuns the thin

    ˋ   ˋ| ˘   ˋ | ˘   ˋ | ˘   ˋ | ˘   ˋ

3. blue air. How odd the mountain first should bring

    ˘   ˋ |˘   ˋ | ˘   ˋ |˘ ˋ| ˘   ˋ

4. the art to mind: impossible to see

    ˘   ˋ | ˘   ˋ|˘ ˋ | ˘   ˋ | ˘   ˋ

5. it free of Hokusai, or you, your lean

    ˘ ˋ|˘   ˋ | ˋ   ˘ |ˋ ˘| ˋ

6. collages—strong, spare—where color swings
    (The "strong, spare" acts like a spondee, but the reversed
    feet together give it that effect. The "swings" is a monosyl-
    labic foot that finishes the requirements of the pentameter
    line.)

˘ ˋ | ˘ ˋ | ˘ ˋ | ˘ ˋ |ˋ ˘

7. its object open like a door. I think

˘ ˋ | ˘ ˋ | ˋ ˋ | ˋ ˋ | ˘ ˘   or
˘ ˋ | ˘ ˋ | ˘ ˋ | ˘ ˋ | ˘ ˘

8. of loves we share: green shades, good gin, Matisse,

˘ ˋ|˘ ˋ|˘ ˋ | ˘ ˘ ˘ ˋ|˘ ˋ

9. the rituals of food. Yet our separate arts
   (As in the following line, the poet seems to pronounce
   "separate" as two syllables which is more colloquial; we
   rarely use three syllables— "sep-ar-ate" — in conversation;
   but we can pronounce the final foot as an anapest.)

˘ ˋ | ˘ ˋ | ˘ ˋ | ˘ ˋ|˘ ˋ

10. define our separate lives. A heron keels
    (Again, the third foot can be an anapest.)

˘ ˋ | ˘ ˋ | ˘ ˋ|˘ ˋ | ˘ ˋ

11. across the Sound. We are absorbed by these

˘ ˋ | ˘ ˋ | ˘ ˋ | ˘ ˋ|˘ ˋ

12. inventions, puzzling mountains into parts

˘ ˋ|˘ ˋ | ˘ ˋ |˘ ˋ| ˘ ˋ

13. until a suddenness of vision yields

˘ ˋ | ˘ ˋ | ˘ ˋ|˘ ˋ | ˘ ˋ

14. a wholeness up: relinquished, we are blessed.

B. **Delight in Disorder**, by Robert Herrick (1648)

˘ ˋ | ˘ ˋ | ˘ ˋ| ˘ ˋ

1. A sweet disorder in the dress

ˋ ˘ | ˘ ˋ |ˋ ˘ | ˘ ˋ

2. Kindles in clothes a wantonness.

˘ ˋ |ˋ ˘ | ˋ ˘ ˋ | ˘ ˋ

3. A lawn about the shoulders thrown

ˋ ˘|ˋ ˋ | ˘ ˋ|˘ ˋ

4. Into a fine distraction
   (This is a problematic line for modern readers; this poem was
   written in the seventeenth century, when the "-tion" was pro-
   nounced as two syllables.)

˘ ˋ | ˘ ˋ | ˘ ˋ | ˘ ˋ

5. An erring lace which here and there

˘ `  |  ˘  ` | ˘ `  |˘  `

6. Enthralls the crimson stomacher

˘ `  |  ˘  `|˘ `  |  ˘  `

7. A cuff neglectful and thereby

`  ˘  |˘  ` |˘ `|˘  `

8. Ribbons to flow confusedly

˘ `  |  ˘  ` | ˘ `|˘  `

9. A winning wave deserving note

`  ˘  |  ˘  `|˘ ˘ `  |˘  `

10. In the tempestuous petticoat

˘ `  |  ˘  ` | ˘ `  |  ˘  `

11. A careless shoestring in whose tie

˘ `  |˘  ` |˘ ˘|˘`

12. I see a wild civility;

˘ `  |  ˘  ` | ˘ `  |  ˘  `

13. Do more bewitch me than when art

˘ `  |  ˘  ˘  |˘  `|˘ `

14. Is too precise in every part.

C. **The Dance (in Breughel's)**, by William Carlos Williams (1944)
(This is a modern poem, which is metrical, but it is not
metrically consistent. Williams uses iambs and anapests to
make the rhythm sound like a dance, but often the feet
overlap from one line to the next.)

˘ `  |  ˘  ˘  `|˘ ˘ ` | ˘

1. In Breughel's great picture, The Kermess,

˘ `  |˘  ˘  ` | ˘ ˘ ` | ˘

2. the dancers go round, they go round and

˘ `  |  ˘  ` |˘ ˘ ` |˘ ˘

3. around, the squeeze and the blare and the

`  |˘˘  `| ˘ ˘ `|˘  ˘  ` | ˘

4. tweedle of bagpipes, a bugle and fiddles

`  ˘  |  ˘  ` |˘ `  |  ˘  ˘  `

5. tipping their bellies (round as the thick-

`  ˘  |  ` ˘| ˘ `  |  ˘  ˘  `

6. sided glasses whose wash they impound)

˘ ˋ | ˘ ˘ ˋ | ˘ ˘ ˋ | ˘

7. their hips and their bellies off balance

˘ ˋ | ˘ ˋ | ˘ ˘ ˋ | ˘ ˘ ˋ

8. to turn them. Kicking and rolling about

˘ ˘ ˋ | ˋ ˘ | ˘ ˋ | ˘   *or*

˘ ˋ | ˋ ˋ | ˘ | ˘ ˋ | ˘

9. the Fair Grounds, swinging their butts, those

ˋ | ˘ ˘ ˋ | ˘ ˘ ˋ | ˋ ˘ ˘

10. shanks must be sound to bear up under such
    (Remember our discussion of phrasal verbs. It sounds as
    though "bear" is stressed, but "bear up" is a phrasal verb
    like "fell down" in "Jack and Jill," and this is written in a
    primarily trisyllabic meter. And the "un-" in "under" gets a
    lexical stress.)

ˋ | ˘ ˘ ˋ | ˘ ˋ | ˘ ˘ ˋ

11. rollicking measures, prance as they dance

˘ ˋ | ˘ ˘ ˋ | ˘ ˘ ˋ | ˘

12. in Breughel's great picture, The Kermess.

D. **One Art**, by Elizabeth Bishop (1976)

˘ ˋ | ˘ ˋ | ˘ ˋ | ˘ ˋ | ˘ ˋ | ˘

1. The art of losing isn't hard to master;

˘ ˋ | ˘ ˋ | ˘ ˋ | ˋ ˘ | ˘ ˋ

2. so many things seem filled with the intent
    (Although "with" is weak, "the" and "in-" are weaker.
    Remember that articles are never stressed. Also, "seem"
    carries less meaning than the syllables around it.)

˘ ˘ | ˋ ˋ | ˘ ˋ | ˋ ˘ ˋ | ˘   *or*
˘ ˋ | ˋ ˘ | ˘ ˋ | ˋ ˘ ˋ | ˘

3. to be lost that their loss is no disaster.
    (This begins with a super-iamb and settles into regular
    iambs.)

ˋ ˋ | ˘ ˋ | ˘ ˋ | ˘ ˋ | ˘ ˋ | ˘

4. Lose something every day. Accept the fluster
    (You may hear the first foot as an iamb, but we should
    agree on the rest.)

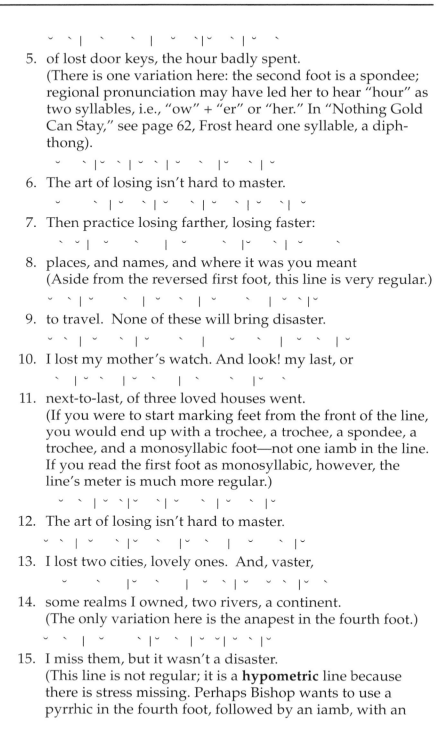

˘ ˋ | ˋ   ˋ | ˘   ˋ|˘   ˋ | ˘   ˋ
5. of lost door keys, the hour badly spent.
   (There is one variation here: the second foot is a spondee;
   regional pronunciation may have led her to hear "hour" as
   two syllables, i.e., "ow" + "er" or "her." In "Nothing Gold
   Can Stay," see page 62, Frost heard one syllable, a diph-
   thong).

   ˘   ˋ |˘   ˋ | ˘   ˋ | ˘   ˋ |˘   ˋ | ˘
6. The art of losing isn't hard to master.

   ˘   ˋ | ˘   ˋ | ˘   ˋ | ˘   ˋ | ˘   ˋ | ˘
7. Then practice losing farther, losing faster:

   ˋ   ˘ | ˘   ˋ | ˘   ˋ |˘   ˋ | ˘   ˋ
8. places, and names, and where it was you meant
   (Aside from the reversed first foot, this line is very regular.)

   ˘   ˋ |˘   ˋ | ˘   ˋ | ˘   ˋ | ˘   ˋ |˘
9. to travel. None of these will bring disaster.

   ˘   ˋ | ˘   ˋ | ˘   ˋ | ˘   ˋ | ˘   ˋ | ˘
10. I lost my mother's watch. And look! my last, or

   ˋ | ˘   ˋ | ˘   ˋ | ˋ   ˋ |˘   ˋ
11. next-to-last, of three loved houses went.
   (If you were to start marking feet from the front of the line,
   you would end up with a trochee, a trochee, a spondee, a
   trochee, and a monosyllabic foot—not one iamb in the line.
   If you read the first foot as monosyllabic, however, the
   line's meter is much more regular.)

   ˘   ˋ | ˘   ˋ|˘   ˋ|˘   ˋ | ˘   ˋ | ˘
12. The art of losing isn't hard to master.

   ˘   ˋ | ˘   ˋ|˘   ˋ |˘   ˋ | ˘   ˋ | ˘
13. I lost two cities, lovely ones. And, vaster,

   ˘   ˋ |˘   ˋ | ˘   ˋ|˘   ˘   ˋ |˘   ˋ
14. some realms I owned, two rivers, a continent.
   (The only variation here is the anapest in the fourth foot.)

   ˘   ˋ | ˘   ˋ |˘   ˋ | ˘   ˘|˘   ˋ |˘
15. I miss them, but it wasn't a disaster.
   (This line is not regular; it is a **hypometric** line because
   there is stress missing. Perhaps Bishop wants to use a
   pyrrhic in the fourth foot, followed by an iamb, with an

unaccented syllable at the end. This would run counter to our belief that pyrrhic feet cannot occur independently. Perhaps she means to metrically illustrate the absence she is speaking of. Perhaps she lost count, or perhaps she wrapped the extra foot into the next line because there are six there. The "a" shouldn't be able to take a stress. Could this be an emphatic "a"? Or is it just an oddity in the line? Any other speculations?)

ˋ| ˘   ˋ | ˘   ˋ | ˘ ˋ| ˘   ˋ | ˘ ˋ | ˘

16. —Even losing you (the joking voice, a gesture
    (This is another strange line. It is a **hypermetric** line be-
    cause it is too long. If you don't look for iambs you will see
    the line as not only long, but also trochaic. There is a lexical
    stress on the first syllable of "Even," so it must be accented.
    But if you follow the version given, most of the line is
    iambic. Yet why the hypermetric line? Perhaps Bishop
    sensed that the hypermetric line balanced the previous
    hypometric line. It could be she wished to loosen up the
    tight demands of the **villanelle** a bit. Although we are
    trying to offer meter as a sensible and simple system, these
    lines present difficulties. This is a great poem, and these
    little variations don't affect the reading rhythm much. We
    don't mind a little pie on our faces now and then.)

˘ ˋ |˘   ˋ | ˘   ˋ | ˘ ˋ|˘ ˋ

17. I love) I shan't have lied. It's evident

˘ ˋ | ˘ ˋ| ˘   ˋ | ˘   ˋ | ˘ ˋ | ˘

18. the art of losing's not too hard to master

˘   ˋ | ˘   ˋ | ˘   ˋ | ˘ ˋ | ˘ ˋ |˘

19. Though it may look like (*Write* it!) like disaster.

E. **Étude**, by A. E. Stallings (2002)

˘ ˋ | ˘ ˋ| ˘   ˋ | ˘   ˋ | ˘ ˋ

1. She fingers it with something like regret,

ˋ | ˘ ˋ |˘   ˋ | ˘   ˘ |˘ ˋ

2. Clasping at its neck, stopping a string

˘   ˋ | ˘ ˋ |˘   ˋ | ˘   ˋ | ˘ ˋ

3. A ghostly music scrapes beneath her ring,

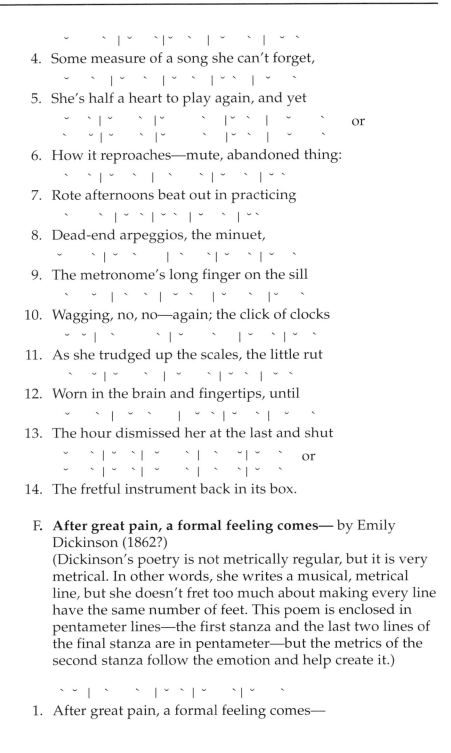

⏑ ˋ | ⏑ ˋ | ⏑ ˋ | ⏑ ˋ | ⏑ ˋ
4. Some measure of a song she can't forget,

⏑ ˋ | ⏑ ˋ | ⏑ ˋ | ⏑ ˋ | ⏑ ˋ
5. She's half a heart to play again, and yet

⏑ ˋ | ⏑ ˋ | ⏑ ˋ | ⏑ ˋ | ⏑ ˋ   or
ˋ ⏑ | ⏑ ˋ | ⏑ ˋ | ⏑ ˋ | ⏑ ˋ
6. How it reproaches—mute, abandoned thing:

ˋ ˋ | ⏑ ˋ | ˋ ˋ | ⏑ ˋ | ⏑ ˋ
7. Rote afternoons beat out in practicing

ˋ ˋ | ⏑ ˋ | ⏑ ˋ | ⏑ ˋ | ⏑ ˋ
8. Dead-end arpeggios, the minuet,

⏑ ˋ | ⏑ ˋ | ˋ ˋ | ⏑ ˋ | ⏑ ˋ
9. The metronome's long finger on the sill

ˋ ⏑ | ˋ ˋ | ⏑ ˋ | ⏑ ˋ | ⏑ ˋ
10. Wagging, no, no—again; the click of clocks

⏑ ⏑ | ˋ ˋ | ⏑ ˋ | ⏑ ˋ | ⏑ ˋ
11. As she trudged up the scales, the little rut

ˋ ⏑ | ⏑ ˋ | ⏑ ˋ | ⏑ ˋ | ⏑ ˋ
12. Worn in the brain and fingertips, until

⏑ ˋ | ⏑ ˋ | ⏑ ˋ | ⏑ ˋ | ⏑ ˋ
13. The hour dismissed her at the last and shut

⏑ ˋ | ⏑ ˋ | ⏑ ˋ | ˋ ⏑ | ⏑ ˋ   or
⏑ ˋ | ⏑ ˋ | ⏑ ˋ | ˋ ⏑ | ⏑ ˋ
14. The fretful instrument back in its box.

F. **After great pain, a formal feeling comes—** by Emily Dickinson (1862?)
(Dickinson's poetry is not metrically regular, but it is very metrical. In other words, she writes a musical, metrical line, but she doesn't fret too much about making every line have the same number of feet. This poem is enclosed in pentameter lines—the first stanza and the last two lines of the final stanza are in pentameter—but the metrics of the second stanza follow the emotion and help create it.)

ˋ ⏑ | ˋ ˋ | ⏑ ˋ | ⏑ ˋ | ⏑ ˋ
1. After great pain, a formal feeling comes—

˘   ˋ | ˋ   ˋ|˘ ˋ | ˘˘ | ˘   ˋ
2. The Nerves sit ceremonious, like Tombs—

˘   ˋ | ˋ   ˋ | ˘   ˋ | ˘   ˋ | ˘   ˋ
3. The stiff Heart questions was it He, that bore,

˘   ˋ | ˘ ˋ | ˘   ˋ | ˘˘ | ˘ ˋ
4. And Yesterday, or Centuries before?

˘   ˋ | ˘   ˋ |˘ ˋ | ˘   ˋ
5. The Feet, mechanical, go round—

˘   ˋ | ˘   ˋ |˘   ˋ
6. Of Ground, or Air, or Ought—

˘   ˋ | ˘   ˋ
7. A Wooden way

˘   ˋ | ˘   ˋ
8. Regardless grown,

˘   ˋ | ˘ ˋ | ˘   ˋ |˘   ˋ
9. A Quartz contentment, like a stone—

ˋ ˘ | ˘   ˋ |˘ ˋ
10. This is the Hour of Lead—

˘   ˋ | ˘   ˋ|˘ ˋ
11. Remembered, if outlived,

˘   ˋ | ˘   ˋ | ˘   ˋ|˘ ˋ | ˘   ˋ
12. As Freezing Persons recollect the Snow—

ˋ   ˋ | ˋ   ˋ|˘   ˋ | ˘ ˋ|˘   ˋ
13. First—Chill—then Stupor—then the letting go.

G. **Aunt Jennifer's Tigers**, by Adrienne Rich (1950)

˘   ˋ | ˘˘   ˋ| ˘ ˋ | ˘˘ | ˘   ˋ
1. Aunt Jennifer's tigers prance across the screen,

ˋ   ˋ | ˘ ˋ|˘ ˋ | ˘ ˘   ˋ |˘   ˋ
2. Bright topaz denizens of a world of green.

˘   ˋ|˘ ˋ | ˘   ˋ | ˘ ˋ | ˘ ˋ
3. They do not fear the men beneath the tree;

˘ ` |˘ ` |˘ ` |˘ `|˘ `
4. They pace in sleek chivalric certainty.

˘ ` | ˘ ˘ ` | ˘ ` |˘˘ ` | ˘ `
5. Aunt Jennifer's fingers fluttering through her wool

` ` | ˘ ˘ `|˘˘ ` | ˘ ` | ˘ `
6. Find even the ivory needle hard to pull.

˘ ` | ˘ ` | ˘ ` | ˘ ` | ˘ `
7. The massive weight of Uncle's wedding band

` ` | ˘ ` | ˘ ` | ˘ ` | ˘˘ `
8. Sits heavily upon Aunt Jennifer's hand.
   (It is possible to see the first foot as an iamb, but the
   spondee emphasizes the heaviness.)

˘ ` | ˘ ` | ˘ ` | ˘ ˘ ` | ˘ `
9. When Aunt is dead, her terrified hands will lie

` ` | ˘ ˘ | ` ` | ˘ ` | ˘ `
10. Still ringed by ordeals she was mastered by.
    (This is the most problematic line; there seems to be a
    missing foot. We argue for a rhetorical stress on "she"; this
    produces a super-iamb in the middle of the line, which,
    while uncommon in iambic meters, is not impossible—and
    preserves the meter.)

˘ ` | ˘ ` | ˘ ` |˘ ` | ˘ `
11. The tigers in the panel that she made

˘ ` | ˘ ` | ˘ ` | ˘ ` |˘ `
12. Will go on prancing, proud and unafraid.
    (The "un-" gets a metrical stress, because of the reader's
    expectation and the weak syllables around it.)

H. **Incident**, by Countee Cullen (1925)

` `| ˘ ` | ` ` | ˘ `
1. Once riding in old Baltimore

` ` | ` ` | ˘ `
2.   Heart-filled, head-filled with glee,

˘ ` | ˘ ` | ` ` | ˘ `
3. I saw a Baltimorean

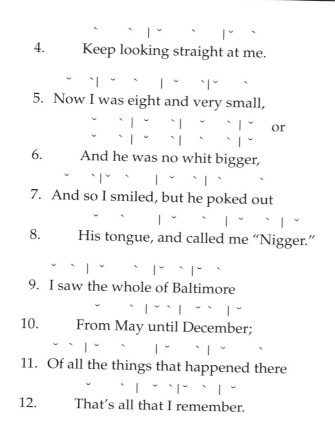

4.   Keep looking straight at me.

5. Now I was eight and very small,

                                                            or

6.   And he was no whit bigger,

7. And so I smiled, but he poked out

8.   His tongue, and called me "Nigger."

9. I saw the whole of Baltimore

10.   From May until December;

11. Of all the things that happened there

12.   That's all that I remember.

13 Sentimentality

When we are considering the merits of any artistic production, we make a distinction between "sentiment" and "sentimentality." The word *sentiment* refers to "the emotional import of a passage as distinguished from the words used." The sentiment in a poem might be the tender regard for a child, anger at war, a love for sensual pleasure, envy of what someone has, or any other network of complex emotion. Determining the sentiment in a poem will help us understand its tone. We view excessive sentiment as being "sentimental," a negative term in literary analysis. By "excessive" we do not mean that the speakers or the poets themselves shouldn't be so in love, so angry, so envious. What we mean is that the writers have not given readers enough background information to feel the same way that they have felt about the child, the war, the pleasure, the object of envy. X. J. Kennedy once wrote that sentimentality results when a writer "implies that he feels great emotion but fails to give us sufficient grounds for sharing it" (1976, 698). We can't say that the writers are being deliberately insincere, because they probably do feel what they say they do. It is just that they have taken a kind of shortcut; they have gone straight to the emotions without acknowledging their readers' need to know what situation or gathering of events the emotion was a result of. Even the poem whose language doesn't seem overripe can be sentimental if the emotion seems misplaced. For example, Rod McKuen has a poem called "Thoughts on Capital Punishment," in which he concludes that people who accidentally run over an animal ought to be killed by "an elephant with an elephant gun"; this trivially misplaces the emotion. His anger at seeing roadkill sponsors a solution which is even more careless than the drivers. In the poem he doesn't mark a distinction between those who might deliberately run over something and those who are mere victims of an unhappy circumstance. His sympathies are with "husbandless does," "fatherless chipmunks," and "Mrs. Badger whose guts lie spilling out" on the highway. This personification is excessive, and the emotion and logic are misplaced. In *From Dawn to Decadence*, Jacques Barzun says "Sentimentality is feeling that shuts out action, real or potential. It is self-centered and a species of make-believe" (2000, 411). McKuen's poem is self-centered because the solution is a species of "make-believe" whose only purpose is to dramatize the delicacy of his own feeling. The poem cannot inspire any real action. Essentially, we are talking about the difference between pity and compassion. Would you rather have someone feel sorry for you or understand the emotions you feel?

One way to view sentimentality is as emotional manipulation. Bad movies often use dramatic moments to make us feel suddenly sad, uplifted, relieved, affirmed. Television sit-coms are especially prone to sentimentality because they operate in such limited time frames that they take shortcuts to emotional content. Song lyrics, greeting cards, children's books, poems, novels, short stories can all be sentimental.

Generally, if the writer is taking shortcuts with the sentiment, then he or she will probably be taking shortcuts on characterization as well. He or she will use a stereotype, some embodiment of our cultural clichés. For example, the poem may consider an old man sitting on the steps in Seattle's Pioneer Square. It may expound upon the ravages of time and a social system that creates outcasts. It may weep over the poor, poor man whose life has bottomed out. Yet what does this poet know of the man himself? Maybe he was an ex-Nazi executioner. Maybe he is a millionaire who likes to slum. Maybe he chooses this life over the demands of mortgage payments and the world of commerce. Maybe he's a laborer who is on a lunch break and will indeed return to a home that is comfortable. Maybe he's a writer doing a book or a story on street life in Seattle. The fact is the sentimental poet or writer doesn't take the time to actually get to know the person, but merely uses him as an excuse to feel bad about the passage of time or unfair social conditions. And it is true that the poet himself or herself probably does feel bad, but the poem hasn't convinced us that we ought to feel the same way.

Consider this sentimental poem, written by Rod McKuen:

The Snow

The snow, the snow keeps on falling
all white like the down of the dove.
The snow, the snow keeps on falling
worthless, like the tears you cry over love.

The lovers promenade like so many sheep
then home they go to the fire's glow
to smile and love and sleep.

And all the snowmen are melting away
the children go again on their way
while the snow, the snow keeps on falling
all white like the down of the dove.

> The snow, the snow keeps on falling
> worthless, like the tears you cry over love.

The sentiment of this poem appears to be sadness caused by some unfulfilled love. It is a general statement and seems to be promoting this feeling as a kind of universal truth. We do not have any specific characters; we only have "lovers," "sheep," "snowmen," and "children." We do not know very precisely how they all interconnect. He repeats the line "the snow, the snow keeps on falling" four times in thirteen lines so that it becomes a kind of refrain. Because it is being compared to the tears we cry over love, we get the sense that every love relationship the writer enters has the same repetitious pattern—it "falls" apart. The comparison of the snow to the "down" of a bird is nicely specific, but why a "dove" in particular? They are not winter birds and tend to migrate away from areas of deep snow. It appears that the dove is merely an easy rhyme with "love" and not included for the accuracy of the comparison. One must also ask why the tears one cries over love are worthless. It is true that they don't bring the missing lover back, but they certainly have a purgative effect—we feel better afterwards. They give us a physical release from inner pain. Surely the poet knows this, but he seems to want to dismiss it in favor of a bitter denunciation of love itself. He seems to be turning his personal frustration into a general condition.

In the second stanza, the **imagery** is not accurate. What does "promenade" mean? According to the *American Heritage Dictionary*, it is a "leisurely walk, especially one taken in a public place as a social activity," and the third definition is "a formal march by the guests at the opening of a ball." So the connotation is that of a walk that is formal and social. Now, these lovers promenade like "sheep." Have you ever seen sheep promenade, hoof linked to hoof in woolly array? After this quaint activity, the lovers go home. Do the lovers have a home? Are they married, living together? Who made the fire? They "smile," and "love, and sleep." Is that all? No conversation, no dinner? No backrubs, no jokes, no signs of mental activity? The poet seems not to care much about the actual lovers; he takes a shortcut to emotional description without providing any context for the reader.

The third stanza introduces snowmen and children, but what do they have to do with the lovers? The snowmen are melting, yet it is still snowing. The children go "again" on "their way." Which way was that and why are they going there again? We perhaps can assume that the children had fun building the snowmen but now have to go home. There doesn't seem to be any clear relationship between the children and the lovers, so we are to take their snowman-building and leaving as parallel to what the lovers are doing—they get together for a time, have fun, and leave. Are all lovers like this? The refrain line of the snow falling and the worthless tears suggests that this is a repeated, cyclical truth. The "tears" suggests that we too ought to cry about this sad predicament. The title of the poem often points toward the central theme or emotion; in this case, "snow" implies that reality is cold and relationships melt away like snowmen. We are not given any reasons for relationships dissolving; it is merely assumed that this is a universal truth, and that they all dissolve in time. Do you believe this? Do you know of any relationships that have survived multiple seasons, years, decades?

McKuen is pointing out a common problem: many relationships fail. But what he doesn't seem to recognize is that he contributes to the problem. His sense of romance is smiling, loving, and sleeping near a fire after a nice promenade in the snow. The poet does not take on the complexity of anyone's love relationship. He presents a poster vision of love where all of the reality has been shaken from the scene and we are left with props.

Now consider the following poem by Joseph Powell.

If, Love

If love had a dark window,
a refuge beyond the sill of doubt,
about which neither pressed to know
and let silence wander in and out,
the rest would assume a clearer light:
a vague suspicion hidden in ink,
an imagined advantage, a moody flight.
We'd know, estranged, what to think.
We'd accept each distant look
that ended a careful speech;
we'd give the other room to walk
the wandered distance back, and reach
out to touch, perhaps, some night
that we cannot know by sight.

The opening sentence of this poem makes a proposition: If love had a dark window, then the "rest" would be clearer. It is almost as if the lover is seen as a house whose lights have not been turned on at night. The window is dark, and its "sill" is doubt. The sill is what holds the window in place, the threshold. The idea is that if love had a "refuge" or some sanctuary that went beyond doubt, accusation, and jealousy, and if both lovers acknowledged these private places without "press[ing] to know" about them, then the "rest" of the difficulties would be easier to bear, easier to deal with. If we allowed our lovers a refuge, an inner privacy that we resolved not to repeatedly violate with questions and suspicions; if we had enough trust, then we would merely wait for the lover to "wander" back to us. We would, instead of prying and accusing, reach out and touch this "night," this dark place in the other, as a kind of comfort and acknowledgment.

The colon at the end of the fifth line suggests that we are given three examples of the kinds of difficulties lovers face. The phrase "vague suspicion hidden in ink" seems to refer to some opportunity for jealousy that one might find in a letter or something that was written. Perhaps a letter arrives from someone out of the past that predated the lover; we tend to demand hasty explanations when perhaps we ought to wait for them. The phrase "imagined advantage" implies that even between couples there is social competition, and when the balance tips we tend to feel inferior or angry. The next phrase, "a moody flight," implies a kind of emotional binge that could have a number of causes—death of a loved one, self-accusations, hormonal swings, whatever. Wouldn't it be more humane to wait for the mood to end before we had it out?

Notice that the title of the poem is "If, Love." Notice too that in the opening two words of the poem the comma is missing. The title then suggests that the poem is conjectural; it is a kind of wish dedicated to the loved one, who is being addressed. The speaker is not saying that their relationship has this kind of refuge, this sanctuary; he is merely saying that if they did have it, then things might be easier.

Both "Snow" and "If, Love" are poems that make a statement about the difficulties of sustaining the love between lovers, but "If, Love" looks more squarely at the difficulties and tries to offer a solution. It doesn't weep and wring its metaphorical hands about the evanescence of love. It doesn't drag the snowmen and children into it, the doves and the sheep.

Sentimental poems not only try to make us sad for no apparent reason, they can also be affirming without looking at complications and contradictions. Here is a poem whose sentimentality is probably a little easier to see. It is by Will Allen Dromgoole (1860–1934); her poems were popular in the early part of the twentieth century.

Old Ladies

In every old lady I chance to meet
    Whoever, wherever she be,
From her snow-crowned head to her patient feet
    My own brave mother I see.

In every old lady whose patient eyes
    Are deeps of a fathomless sea,
So patient and tender and kind and wise
    My mother looks out at me.

In every old lady in silent prayer
    To God on her bended knee,
I vision my own mother kneeling there
    Praying a prayer for me.

In every old lady I bend above,
    Asleep in death's mystery,
I whisper, "Please carry my lone heart's love
    To my angel mother for me."

In every old lady I meet each day
    The humble, or lofty and fine,
I see an angel stand, guarding the way,
    Somebody's mother and mine.

We cannot doubt the sincerity of the sentiment in this poem. Clearly, the poet feels the loss of her mother very deeply. And for family members who knew the mother, this might be a moving poem. But for general readers who know nothing of the speaker or her mother, we feel not pathos but bathos (i.e., insincere pathos, mawkishness). There is a difference between private and public poems. Private poems are written for a loved one to show how one feels about another; it can be to a parent, a lover, a sibling, a friend. It is meant for one or two pairs of eyes only. The poet doesn't have to provide the context, the reasons, the background information, because the mother, lover, brother, or friend knows the context already. They have common experiences and one word might be sufficient to recall a whole vacation, a romantic dinner, or any other shared event. But that one word is not sufficient for a wider audience who did not participate in those experiences. So if a poet has ambitions to write for a broader, more general audience, then he or she is obliged to fill in the context, to give his or her arguments support, to illustrate his or her points—as one would do in an essay.

"Old Ladies" is a private poem that might make a good eulogy at a funeral, but as a public poem it has failed to attend to the readers' need to know more about the mother so that we care about her as well. The speaker says that her mother is "patient," "brave," "tender," "kind," and "wise," and that her eyes are "deeps of a fathomless sea." Yet there is no proof or illustration for any of these judgments. What brave thing did she do? How did she exhibit her kindness? What acts or advice were wise? Why did her eyes seem so "fathomless" or so "deep"? We can assume from the third stanza that the mother liked to pray, but that is the only detail we have about her.

The meter and strategies of the poem also indicate sentimentality. If we look at the meter of the second stanza, we feel the light lilting energy of the anapests, which is more appropriate for a dance or a tale like "The Night before Christmas." The form of the poem is four-line stanzas with the first and third lines in tetrameter and the second and fourth in trimeter, and it is rhymed *abab.* This is often called **common meter**, designated in old hymnals with *C.M.* The anapests and the end-stopped lines give a lightness to the tone that contradicts the sentiment of the speaker. Every line in the poem has one or two anapests, and the rest of the meter is very predictable, aside from a couple spondees in the penultimate stanza. The strategy of repeating "In every old lady" at the beginning of every stanza implies a lack of verbal ingenuity, compounds the overgeneralization, and creates an easy solution to a complex problem. The problem here is the loss of the speaker's mother, yet "In every old lady I chance to meet / Whoever, wherever she be" the speaker sees her own mother, regardless of whether the lady she sees is "humble, or lofty and fine." Is it really plausible that *every* old lady suggests her mother? This attitude refuses to acknowledge the individual value of the old women, their unique sets of circumstances and life choices. They automatically get transformed into the speaker's mother. There is an unsavory solipsism in this attitude—the whole world becomes a kind of church for the speaker's grief. The little prayer the speaker whispers over dead women also asks for the reader's sympathy without really earning it: "my lone heart's love." The three stresses make emphatic an already sentimental line. The "lone" emphasizes her abandonment, and we are to take pity on her because of it. If her mother was old, "snow-crowned," and angelic in her life, why wouldn't her death be a more joyous occasion—if the Christian religious values expressed in the poem are sincere? Wouldn't the speaker's mother be in heaven now?

This also brings up the issue of poems that illustrate the ethics, morality, or temperament of particular groups who would be predisposed to accept the values demonstrated in the poem. A poem that presents a standard Christian, Muslim, Buddhist, Hindu, Native American, or Jewish perspective has as its audience members of that particular group. Poets who do not have a broader sense of audience often use shortcuts—either through imagery or recognizable statement—to appeal to like-minded believers. A poem that uses standard Christian imagery and was written to be published in a Christian magazine should not be expected to be of interest to people outside that belief system. Sentimental poems in this category would also include cowboy, nature, New Age, erotic, queer, or feminist poetry whose intention is merely to congratulate a point of view.

There are ways to write about one's mother as well as ways to write from a particular ideological or personal perspective without being sentimental. One does this by creating new and engaging imagery, being wary about the application of the values projected, being wary of invoking stereotypes, and being aware that people and the solutions to human problems are very complex. Consider the following two poems; the first was written by Judson Mitcham in 1996; the second by Gerard Manley Hopkins in 1877.

An Introduction

You who break the dark all night, whisper and shout,
who travel in and out of all the rooms,
who come with pill or needle, vial or chart,
with bedding, mop and bucket, tray of food;
who turn, clean, pull, read, record, pat, and go;
who see her hair matted by the pillow, greasy white
wild short hair that will shock
anyone from home who hasn't seen her for a while—
shocking like her bones, showing now,
like plum-colored bruises on her arms, like her face
when she first comes to and what it says, like her mouth
and the anything it says: *Call the bird dogs*, or
I've got to go to school, or *Tonight y'all roll*
that wagon wheel all the way to Mexico; you
who have seen three children—unbelieving, unresigned—
in all these rooms, full of anger and of prayer;
you who change her diaper, empty pans

of green and gold bile she has puked up; you
who cannot help breathing her decay,

I would like to introduce you to our mother,
who was beautiful, her eyes like nightshade,
her wavy brown hair with a trace of gold. Myrtle,
whose alto flowed through the smooth
baritone our father used to sing;
our mother, who would make us cut a switch,
but who rocked us and who held us and who kissed us;
Myrtle, wizard typist, sharp with figures,
masterful with roses and with roast beef;
who worked for the New Deal Seed Loan Program,
for the school, local paper, county agent, and the church;

who cared long years for her own failing mother
(whom she worries for now—you may have heard her);
who was tender to a fault, maybe gullible,
as the truly good and trusting often are; and even so,
who could move beyond fools, though foolishness itself
delighted her—a double take, words turned around,
a silly dance—and when our mother laughed
(I tell you this because you haven't heard it),
the world could change, as though the sun could shine
inside our very bones.
                                    And where it's written in Isaiah
that the briar won't rise, but the myrtle tree,
there's a promise unfulfilled:
she will not go out with joy.
Still, if you had known her, you yourselves,
like Isaiah's hills, would sing. You'd understand
why it says *all the trees*
of the field shall clap their hands.

Pied Beauty

Glory be to God for dappled things—
For skies of couple-color as a brinded cow;
    For rose-moles all in stipple upon trout that swim;
Fresh-firecoal chestnut-falls; finches' wings;
Landscape plotted and pieced—fold, fallow, and plow;
    And all trades, their gear and tackle and trim.
All things counter, original, spare, strange;

> Whatever is fickle, freckled (who knows how?)
> With swift, slow; sweet, sour; adazzle, dim;
> He fathers-forth whose beauty is past change:
> Praise Him.

In the first poem, the poet presents "An Introduction" to his mother. He recognizes that a full, complete description of his mother is probably impossible. We are always more complex than the details in any description, but at least we can isolate salient features and build a composite picture, an introduction. We certainly know more about Myrtle than the mother presented in "Old Ladies." From the poet's description in the first two stanzas, we know that he is dedicated to telling the truth: the mother has "greasy white" hair, smells of "decay," has "plum-colored bruises," and babbles sometimes. Because he is concerned that the staff at the hospital or nursing home will see his mother as just another incoherent patient and judge her negatively, he wishes to give them a fuller context, to turn the wrinkles into a real person. The details about her life seem carefully chosen and deliberately positive, but his adherence to the truth reveals edges of her personality, which aren't completely good (as no one ever is). So besides being a "wizard typist," a loving mother, "masterful with roses" and "roast beef," a socially conscious citizen, and beautiful, she made her children "cut a switch" for their own punishment, liked "foolishness," and was a little "gullible." The details are specific enough that we get a sense of who she is, a real introduction.

In Hopkins's poem, the details are so fresh, the language so engaging, that even the most convinced atheist would have to admit that Hopkins had written a great poem. The atheist may not be persuaded by the argument to change his or her religious attitudes, but he or she certainly would have more respect for Hopkins's views. Hopkins has given eloquent reasons for his belief—the glorious multitude of "dappled things" in the world suggests to him a marvelous and grand creator. By forcing us to look closely at the world, especially at things we may have overlooked, he has composed a passionate argument. The images of clouds like spots on a cow, the "rose-moles" of trout, the spotted wings of some finches are so particular and visually accurate that we accept Hopkins's evidence. And he doesn't just praise natural phenomena, but the human world as well— "all trades, their gear and tackle and trim." He loves "all things" that are original and strange, but his little bit of doubt ("who knows how") allows the doubters a place at the table. These skeptics aren't browbeaten by a smug surety, but welcomed and invited to join the feast.

No matter where we ascribe the ultimate value and meaning in the universe—whether to God, Nature, Accident, Buddha, Allah—our experience in the world is deepened a little by this poem. Poems that baldly state one's faith without exhibiting the causes for this fervor, or demonstrating it through details, are going to seem sentimental to people who do not share the poet's or speaker's attitudes. The writer of "Old Ladies" assumes that the mere mentioning of praying and angels is enough to garner emotional support for the poem's point of view.

To further demonstrate how meter can compound sentimentality, we would like to provide another example. The sentimental poet often seems to believe that meter intensifies the feeling of the poem. Quite often, however, such a poet lacks technical skill and his or her weaknesses with imagery, grammatical structure, and precision are simply intensified by meter and rhyme. Here are the final eight lines of a poem titled "My Little Brother," by the British poet David Gray:

> Let the curtain rest; for alas! 't is told
> That Mercy's hand benign
> Hath woven and spun the gossamer thread
> That forms the fabric so fine.
> Then dream, dearest Jackie! thy sinless dream,
> And waken as blithe and as free;
> There's many a change in twenty long years,
> My brown little brother of three.

In this poem the faults are not glaring. It is unclear whether the poem is a meditation on a brother who has died or on the changes the child will experience over the next twenty years. That confusion also suggests a lack of skill, for we ought to know whether the child is dead or alive. In the lines quoted, you'll notice a good deal of needless repetition and insistence. Could "Mercy" and her personified "hand" be anything but "benign"? Is a fabric "so fine" better than one that's just "fine"? The "so" is an empty intensifier used merely to create an anapest. Isn't it odd to mention "woven" before "spun"—don't you need to spin thread before you can weave it? Why "little" in "little brother of three"? If he is three, he is little. The two exclamation points add a bit of unearned emotional drama (as they often do in bad poems). Lack of precision and unnecessary emphasis are signs of bad writing.

The presence of sentimentality is signaled partly by the subject matter—a little brother who may or may not be alive; partly by the use of emotionally loaded words like "alas" and "dearest"; partly by hackneyed language like "gossamer thread"; and partly by the meter. The problem is that anapestic meter has so strong a lilt to it that it's not well suited to serious, much less solemn, writing. The poem skips along, which is fine when it describes the child scampering in the country, but then it continues to skip when the speaker asks troubling questions. In this poem, the choice of meter is also at odds with the emotionally intensifying words. Because of the strong stress requirements in anapestic meters, both "dearest" and "little" have to be read as if they had no accents. The words are supposed to be submerged under the heavier accents in "Jackie" and "brother." In the penultimate line, "long" is also submerged to be part of the anapestic foot, and thus the poet has missed the opportunity of metrically emphasizing or "accenting" the length of time that will elapse and test Mercy's hand—one of the main points of the poem. The poem's thematic concern is how time flies, how short-lived and carefree youth is. These solemn thoughts demand a rich, full resonance. Rather than using the tones of an organ, however, the poet plays with a xylophone. When the tune and the instrument on which it's played are mismatched, the effect can generate unintentional humor, a trap into which the sentimentalist frequently falls.

See if you can determine which of the following poems are sentimental and why.

1. Channing Way, 2

I should have told you
that love is more
            than being warm in bed.
                                    More
than individuals seeking an accomplice.
Even more than wanting to share.

I could have said
that love at best is giving what you need to get.

But it was raining
and we had no place to go
and riding through the streets in a cab
                        I remembered
that words are only necessary after love has gone.

2. My Mother

Who fed me from her gentle breast
And hushed me in her arms to rest,
And on my cheek sweet kisses prest?
            My mother.

When sleep forsook my open eye,
Who was it sung sweet lullaby
And rocked me that I should not cry?
     My mother.

When pain and sickness made me cry,
Who gazed upon my heavy eye
And wept, for fear that I would die?
     My mother.

Who ran to help me when I fell
And would some pretty story tell,
Or kiss the part to make it well?
     My mother.

Who taught my infant lips to pray,
To love God's holy word and day,
And walk in wisdom's pleasant way?
     My mother.

And can I ever cease to be
Affectionate and kind to thee
Who wast so very kind to me,—
     My mother.

Oh no, the thought I cannot bear;
And if God please my life to spare
I hope I shall reward thy care,
     My mother.

When thou art feeble, old and gray,
My healthy arm shall be thy stay,
And I will soothe the pains away,
     My mother.

And when I see thee hang thy head,
'Twill be my turn to watch thy bed,
And tears of sweet affection shed,—
     My mother.

3. Piano

Softly, in the dusk, a woman is singing to me;
Taking me back down the vista of years, till I see
A child sitting under the piano, in the boom of the tingling strings
And pressing the small, poised feet of a mother who smiles as
   she sings.

In spite of myself, the insidious mastery of song
Betrays me back, till the heart of me weeps to belong
To the old Sunday evenings at home, with winter outside
And hymns in the cosy parlour, the tinkling piano our guide.

So now it is vain for the singer to burst into clamour
With the great black piano appassionato. The glamour
Of childish days is upon me, my manhood is cast
Down in the flood of remembrance, I weep like a child for the past.

4. The Sands of Dee

"Oh Mary, go and call the cattle home,
    And call the cattle home,
    And call the cattle home,
Across the sands of Dee!"
The western wind was wild and dank with foam,
  And all alone went she.

The western tide crept up along the sand,
    And o'er and o'er the sand,
    And round and round the sand
  As far as eye could see.
The rolling mist came down and hid the land:
  And never home came she.

"Oh! Is it weed, or fish, or floating hair—
    A tress of golden hair,
    A drowned maiden's hair
  Above the nets at sea?
Was never salmon yet that shone so fair
  Among the stakes on Dee."

They rowed her in across the rolling foam,
    The cruel, crawling foam,
    The cruel, hungry foam,
  To her grave beside the sea:
But still the boatmen hear her call the cattle home
  Across the sands of Dee.

("Channing Way, 2" was written by Rod McKuen; "My Mother," by Jane Taylor; "Piano," by D. H. Lawrence; "The Sands of Dee," by Charles Kingsley.)

14 Writing about Poems

There are a number of strategies for writing about poems and poets. Because most introduction-to-poetry courses are taught from an anthology, there are fewer opportunities to look at how ideas or imagery typically develop in a book of poems by one author. But if you did read a book, you could ask a question about recurring ideas or images and attempt to answer it by looking closely at all the poems that dealt with that issue or those images. For example, if you had read Lisel Mueller's *Alive Together,* a few of the questions you might pose at the end could begin to examine her attitudes about music versus writing; how we might characterize her feminism; how we might define the nature of her spirituality—how conventional and how individual it is; and how she dealt with her German heritage and the Holocaust. To write a paper that attempts to come to terms with one of these ideas, you must collect all the poems that deal directly or indirectly with the issue.

Then you must read them all and try to synthesize the material. After examining and doodling or whatever prewriting strategy you use, try to make an assertion that seems true. This assertion is called a thesis. For example, one might make this claim about her spirituality: "Although Mueller does not seem to be consoled by a Christian sense of afterlife, she feels that there are deeper forms of reality that we can't fully know or apprehend and that love and the memories of survivors give us something to believe in and provide some hope." This would be an adequate thesis that one could then set about proving. It has several parts and the writer would have to consider each part and prove it. There are poems that say rather directly that she doesn't believe in an afterlife; there are poems that depict a hyperreality that seems to coexist with the one we perceive; there are poems that illustrate the power of love, especially when one is faced with the loss of a parent or friend; there are poems that use memory to evoke the characters of loved ones as well as poems that directly discuss the role of memory. The writer of this paper would have to prove his or her thesis by discussing aspects of each of these poem types; he or she would then have to quote and analyze the appropriate passages. A writer who had taken on another question would have to go through the same process of gathering relevant poems, arriving at a thesis, and proving that thesis.

However, because anthologies rarely include enough poems by one poet to do this kind of essay, we will consider another kind of assignment: the **explication** of one poem. To *explicate* literally means to "unfold or expand," "to unfold what is wrapped up." So what you are doing is opening up the poem, unfolding it so that the reader can see its subtlest manifestations. One of the definitions of "explication" in the *Oxford English Dictionary* is "the action or process of removing difficulty or obscurity from, or making clear the meaning of." The writer's job then is to "remove the difficulty" of reading the poem, to eliminate what may at first seem obscure.

It is possible to write a paper solely on the metrical effects in a poem, but you would also have to deal with the content and how the metrical choices amplify or help define that content. Because you are just learning to scan, we think it is more useful to be able to spot the most important metrical effects and to incorporate them into your explication. Generally, you must pay close attention to the variations because that is where meaning shifts or is emphasized in various ways.

In an explication essay, you would demonstrate a detailed reading and analysis of a poem in all of its complexity—ideas, argumentative strategies, linguistic choices, metaphors, and metrical effects. Typically, you proceed by examining the poem line by line or stanza by stanza and explaining each part as completely as you can, showing how the poet's techniques produced your response.

The first obstacle to writing a good explication is choosing the poem. If the poem is too brief or obvious, then there is very little to do. It would be like telling your audience how to make toast or boil eggs. Poems that are obvious after a couple of readings are not necessarily inferior to more complex poems. Simplicity and directness have their charms and are often preferable to obliqueness, and may be more profound, but for an explication there needs to be some "difficulty" to remove, some "obscurity" to clarify. The poem must be complicated enough to warrant the attention you give it. However, if the poem is too ornate, complicated, and long, then you are burdened by many possibilities and obligations. Explicating *Paradise Lost,* by John Milton, or "The Blue Guitar," by Wallace Stevens, in a 1,000- to 1,500-word essay would not be wise.

It is best if you can find a poem that allows divergent interpretations; then you can argue for one and against the other. For example, Theodore Roethke's "My Papa's Waltz" is a narrative from a boy's point of view. You will find the poem and an analysis of its meter on pages 19–26. There are two possible interpretations of this poem: one reading sees it as a love poem to the speaker's father, and assumes that Roethke is speaking for himself as a child; the other sees it as a poem about a parent's abuse of a child. The one the reader chooses is often influenced by his or her experience. How we view a poem often depends on how predisposed we are to like its subject matter, its tone, its descriptions, its observations, its characters, its conclusions. But there is no "correct" interpretation; it all depends on how well you argue your case.

How do we argue that the boy is really having a good time, despite his scraped ear and the time "beat" out on his head? Despite his frowning mother and the fact that he is, at the end of the poem, "clinging" to his father's shirt? One useful strategy is to begin by considering the poem in the context of the book it comes from. We can go to the library and find out that the poem was first published and copyrighted in 1942 by Hearst Magazines, Inc., and that it first appeared in a collection of poems in 1948 called *The Lost Son and Other Poems*. There are a number of greenhouse poems in this collection that recall, from a child's point of view, the world of flowers, soil, water, glass, and his father's work. The poems that mention the father are sometimes ambivalent, but are, generally, affirmative and admiring.

It is often important to see where and how a poem fits into a particular collection because poets take great pains to arrange poems so that they talk to each other. One only has to think of William Blake's *Songs of Innocence* and *Songs of Experience* to understand this point. One cannot fully appreciate the deliberate naïveté in the innocence section unless one has also read the poems about experience. So when Roethke follows the greenhouse section of poems with "My Papa's Waltz," he is implying that it shares allegiance with the first section and provides a transition into the second. Of course, all this is outside the poem in the anthology, but the volume the poem comes from is easy enough to find in a library.

Next, the writer must look carefully at the poem itself: its tone, its waltzing meter, its imagery (the whiskey breath making the boy dizzy, holding on "like death"), and its word choices (like "beat," "unfrown," "countenance," "clinging"). Your obligation would be to "explain" the imagery and word choices in the context of a love poem.

The second interpretation sees the poem as illustrating a drunk's abuse of an innocent child. In this case, we might emphasize the whiskey, the holding on "like death," the pans falling, the mother's irritation, the "battered" knuckle of the father, the scraped ear, the way the father "beat" time on the boy's head, the dirty hand, and the child "clinging" to his father's shirt. Library research might acquaint the writer with more information about Roethke's relationship to his father and Roethke's own drinking, both of which might have made him less sensitive to the actual level of "abuse" in the poem. The more positive image of alcohol in America during the early 1940s, an era that valorized drinking cocktails and smoking, might be also brought to bear. It might be helpful to alert readers that nothing was known of fetal alcohol syndrome or drunk-driving statistics during an era that hid abuse and touted the use of the rod as the antidote to spoiling the child.

Whichever stance you take, you have to be aware that a reader can have a different interpretation, and, thus, you must try to anticipate objections the reader might make to your points. This can be done as you consider ambiguous words in your explication, or words that could possibly be misconstrued or misinterpreted. You can deal with these issues in a paragraph of counterarguments just before your conclusion, or you can deal with them along the way as you go through the poem. It should be clear that one will get more mileage out of a poem that can accommodate more than one interpretation.

Because most poems can't sustain such divergent points of view, you often must choose a poem that is difficult; you have to then "unfold" it for the reader, to open it to view. It is something of a myth that poems are only what you make of them. "My Papa's Waltz" is not about a composer's son; it is not about the greenhouse effect; it is not about a dance teacher. Poems usually have very specific topics and specific treatments of those topics. Readers may feel differently about the poem or get distracted by their own private associations, but the poem does what it does and says what it says. One of the reasons Roethke's poem is ambiguous is that there is a distance between the speaker as an adult remembering his childhood, and the speaker "still clinging" to this father's shirt. The attitude toward the event is ambiguous in the speaker's mind. A good reading of the poem will reflect this ambiguity. The writer who sees a love poem must acknowledge the "scraped" ear, and the writer who sees alcohol abuse must acknowledge the boy's excitement.

Generally, the argument that any interpretation of a poem is valid is made by people who feel intimidated by poetry and wish only to dismiss it as something irrelevant, a waste of time, a contrary nuisance. If the poem can mean anything, then these people can't be wrong—no matter how little effort they put into reading and interpreting it. "Interpreting" a poem should presuppose an "active" reading, one in which the reader looked up all the words, reread the poem, and thought hard about the meanings of the **figurative language**. Poems are essentially little explosions of meaning; their purpose is to communicate something to someone. To dismiss them by saying any interpretation is valid also dismisses hours, months, and years of work by people dedicated to communicating something rather specific to a reader. Good readers know that all poems are not created equal, that each has its own story to tell. The best explications preserve the integrity of the poem under analysis by trying to be fair, by telling the truth, by not conveniently overlooking evidence that contradicts the interpretation being offered.

So when you look for a poem to analyze, you should make sure you have enough to consider—complex metaphors, counterarguments, an interpretation that may seem to the casual reader to be somewhat unorthodox, intriguing **diction** choices, and interesting metrical effects to explore. Read the following poem by Richard Wilbur and consider its potential for an essay, then read the student's essay about it, and think about his strategies for setting up his argument and how he proves his points.

The Writer

In her room at the prow of the house
Where light breaks, and the windows are tossed with linden,
My daughter is writing a story.

I pause in the stairwell, hearing
From her shut door a commotion of typewriter-keys
Like a chain hauled over a gunwale.

Young as she is, the stuff
Of her life is a great cargo, and some of it heavy:
I wish her a lucky passage.

But now it is she who pauses,
As if to reject my thought and its easy figure.
A stillness greatens, in which

The whole house seems to be thinking,
And then she is at it again with a bunched clamor
Of strokes, and again is silent.

I remember the dazed starling
Which was trapped in that very room, two years ago;
How we stole in, lifted a sash

And retreated, not to affright it;
And how for a helpless hour, through the crack in the door,
We watched the sleek, wild, dark

And iridescent creature
Batter against the brilliance, drop like a glove
To the hard floor, or the desk-top

And wait then, humped and bloody,
For the wits to try it again; and how our spirits
Rose when, suddenly sure,

It lifted off from a chair-back,
Beating a smooth course for the right window
And clearing the sill of the world.

It is always a matter, my darling,
Of life or death, as I had forgotten. I wish
What I wished you before, but harder.

This essay was written by Sechin Tower, a student in one of our classes. Notice how he works his way through Wilbur's poem, how he uses quotations and makes them part of his sentences, and how he talks about the metrical aspects of the poem.

Love and Understanding in Richard Wilbur's "The Writer"

The narrative context of Richard Wilbur's "The Writer" is quite simple: the speaker listens as his daughter types a story. He thinks first of a ship on a voyage and then, after a pause, of a bird that was once trapped in her room. The emotional import of the poem, however, does not dwell in the course of events as much as it does in the ruminations of the father that show him to possess both a deep love for and a respectful understanding of his daughter. He wants to do what is best for her, but he knows that at this time what is best is to allow her to find her own way to express herself.

This poem is most aptly described as a muse poem, whether one defines "muse" as the act of being absorbed in one's thoughts, as the speaker does while listening to his daughter type, or defines "muse" as a source of inspiration, as his daughter provides for this work. Muses come in many forms: to the ancient Greeks (with whom the term originated) the muses were nine divine sisters, each of whom inspired certain types of artwork in mortals. In William Wordsworth's poem "The Solitary Reaper," the muse takes the shape of a "highland lass" whose work song inspires and intrigues travelers as they pass by. In contrast to the very personal parent-child relationship of "The Writer," Wordsworth's muse is a stranger, but her song creates a personal connection with him and reverberates in the regular meter and rhyme of that poem.

"The Writer" draws upon a literary rather than a musical muse, and perhaps this is why it has a much less rhythmic sound than many other metrical poems. The stanzas are composed of un-rhymed tercets, the first line of each consisting of three metrical feet, the second of five feet, and the third of three feet. While anapests are the predominant metrical foot, there are a great number of variations in every stanza—in the ninth stanza, for example, the uncertain atmosphere in which the battered starling prepares for another attempt at flight is supported by the fact that only three of the stanza's eleven feet are anapests. Almost every stanza also contains spondees, which are used to embolden the images to which they are attached. As the poem opens, these spondees bring a sense of potency to the boat as it pushes its way through the ocean, making the "chain hauled over a gunwale" and the "great cargo" seem very heavy indeed. Later, the intrigue of the starling is boldly described in the three consecutive accented syllables "sleek, wild, dark," a description made all the more striking by the fact that they end the stanza in an incomplete sentence. Spondees also lend the objects which the starling interacts with a strength of their own, reminding us that the "hard floor," the "desk top," and the "chair back" are very hard, real things that the small starling must overcome. The starling's escape is also celebrated with spondees, as the bird finally finds a "smooth course" which takes him through the "right window."

The most interesting poetic devices used by Wilbur are not those of meter, but of metaphor, which are evoked from the first line of the poem onward. This line establishes the spatial focus of this poem as being "in her room," but also describes her room as being "at the prow of the house." A prow is the forward part of a ship, in this case symbolizing that she is in the foremost position in the household, that wherever the family may be heading, she will lead the way. All of the first three stanzas utilize the extended metaphor of the ship: her room is "where light breaks" (as waves break on the prow), the commotion of her typewriter keys sounds "like a chain hauled over a gunwale," the stuff of her life is a "great cargo," and her father wishes her a "lucky passage." This metaphor proves to be fitting, demonstrating that the father knows what the daughter is going through—her life is a journey and she has already accumulated very valuable "cargo" which she can deliver only through writing, her chosen form of self-expression.

When the daughter pauses at her typewriter, the father comes out of his reverie and the metaphor of the ship dissolves. In the growing quiet he realizes that his "thought and its easy figure" (meaning the metaphor of the ship) was merely a flight of fancy, and he waits—almost in suspense—for his daughter to resume. The stillness is not a void, but rather a pregnant pause "in which / the whole house seems to be thinking." This is how the writing process goes—a fit of creation followed by reflection in which metaphors and other devices are revised and reconsidered.

The speaker does not know (and may never know) what new thoughts the daughter developed during the pause, but as she cycles through periods of rapid typing and silent pause, the speaker begins to explore the second extended metaphor of the poem. While the ship was an abstract comparison, lumbering and distant, the speaker now recalls the living, breathing, beautiful image of the "dazed starling" which was trapped not on some distant imaginary sea, but "in that very room." This metaphor is also presented in a different way than the previous one: whereas the ship was made in comparison to the daughter's life, the starling develops as a subnarrative within the body of this work. One might miss the use of the starling as a metaphor altogether, taking it instead simply to be a literal memory of that room. But, while there is no reason to doubt that a starling had been trapped there (a perfectly realistic experience), this description takes on a much greater significance when considered within the context of the speaker's preoccupation with his daughter throughout the poem—the father's thoughts revolve around his daughter and his contemplation of the bird is not an aside to his contemplation of her, but a development of it. After all, the title of the poem is "The Writer," and not "The Writer and the Bird" or "The Writer's Room."

Thinking about a bird trapped in a room is a good way to understand the confusion and frustration felt by most young adults: they know that there is a wide world outside of the confines of their current life, but they are not sure how to connect to it. In this case, the starling becomes a representation of the artistic impulse within the daughter, struggling to take flight and be free, only to be rebuffed again and again as it seeks the "right window." The speaker of this poem wants very much for his daughter to come into her own, but he knows that direct intervention would only undermine her journey of personal creativity. Instead, his strategy is that of indirect assistance: "we stole in, lifted a sash / and retreated, not to frighten it." For the daughter, the "lifting of the sash" would be her introduction to writing as a means of self-expression, as well as a more general course of action intended to help her see her own freedom.

After the means to enter the world is provided for the bird, there is nothing more to do but to step out and watch. To the speaker, the bird, is, as a source of wonder and inspiration, simultaneously "sleek, wild, dark" and "iridescent." Any parents will feel a similar fascination when they first realize that their children have grown to the point where they have their own lives and ideas. Unfortunately, this is not a painless process, and children may hurt themselves during their self-discovery, just as the bird flies into the wrong window to "batter against the brilliance, drop like a glove . . . and wait then, humped and bloody, for the wits to try it again." One might feel the impulse to grab the bird and force it out the window, but the fragile, furious little creature is likely to injure itself fighting against the hands of its would-be saviors. The same is true for children: at some point children must also be allowed to choose their own ways and make their own mistakes, even if they make some bad choices along the way. The speaker of this poem knows this, and, as much as he might want to go into the room to help, he does not try to write his daughter's story for her any more than he would try to force the bird out the window. The pain and struggle of the bird and the daughter are not in vain: just as the spirits of the onlookers are raised as the bird finally finds the right window to free itself, so too will parents feel elation when they see their children come into their own, successfully "leaving the nest" as the cliché goes. Success for this daughter comes in the form of her writing, which, when it finally comes together, acts as the wings that enable her to lift from her chair and fly free, smoothly "clearing the sill of the world."

The last stanza drops all metaphors so that the speaker can express the compassion he feels for his daughter in a very clear, simple, and colloquial manner. In the third stanza he wished her a "lucky passage" in her experiences of life (as well as in her writing), and the last line wishes her the same again, "but harder." He does not wish her a smooth passage—he knows that flying through the right window on the first attempt is not always what serves a person best. Instead, he wishes her a "lucky" passage, because he hopes that she will make herself into what he knows he cannot make her, and that in time she will find her own ways to enjoy all that life has to offer. While he cannot know what muse sings to her as she types, she acts as his muse while he listens, inspiring him by reminding him of everything that he was at that age, when all matters were "of life or death," and the words surged in his head, looking to take form through writing just as a bird looks for freedom through an open window.

Poem Appendix

The following is a sequence of poems or excerpts from longer poems on which you can practice your scansion. Scan the poems, find the dominant foot, and the variations (if there are any).

A. This is the first stanza of a long poem called "The Anniad," by Gwendolyn Brooks (1949).

1. Think of sweet and chocolate,
2. Left to folly or to fate,
3. Whom the higher gods forgot,
4. Whom the lower gods berate;
5. Physical and underfed
6. Fancying on the featherbed
7. What was never and is not.

B. **Museum Piece**, by Richard Wilbur (1950)

1. The good gray guardians of art
2. Patrol the halls on spongy shoes,
3. Impartially protective, though
4. Perhaps suspicious of Toulouse.

5. Here dozes one against the wall,
6. Disposed upon a funeral chair.
7. A Degas dancer pirouettes
8. Upon the parting of his hair.

9. See how she spins! The grace is there,
10. But strain as well is plain to see.
11. Degas loved the two together:
12. Beauty joined to energy.

13. Edgar Degas purchased once
14. A fine El Greco, which he kept
15. Against the wall beside his bed
16. To hang his pants on while he slept.

C. **Juan's Song**, by Louise Bogan (1923)

1. When beauty breaks and falls asunder
2. I feel no grief for it, but wonder.
3. When love, like a frail shell, lies broken,
4. I keep no chip of it for token.

   5. I never had a man for friend
   6. Who did not know that love must end.
   7. I never had a girl for lover
   8. Who could discern when love was over.
   9. What the wise doubt, the fool believes—
  10. Who is it, then, that love deceives?

   D. **Rondeau,** by Leigh Hunt (1838)

   1. Jenny kiss'd me when we met,
   2.   Jumping from the chair she sat in;
   3. Time, you thief, who love to get
   4.   Sweets into your list, put that in:
   5. Say I'm weary, say I'm sad,
   6.   Say that health and wealth have miss'd me,
   7. Say I'm growing old, but add,
   8.   Jenny kiss'd me.

   E. **So We'll Go No More A-Roving**, by George Gordon, Lord Byron (1817)

   1. So, we'll go no more a-roving
   2.   So late into the night,
   3. Though the heart be still as loving,
   4.   And the moon be still as bright.

   5. For the sword outwears its sheath,
   6.   And the soul wears out the breast,
   7. And the heart must pause to breathe
   8.   And love itself have rest.

   9. Though the night was made for loving,
  10.   And the day returns too soon,
  11. Yet we'll go no more a-roving
  12.   By the light of the moon.

   F. **The Moon**, by Percy Bysshe Shelley (1820)

       I.
   1. And, like a dying lady lean and pale,
   2. Who totters forth, wrapp'd in a gauzy veil,
   3. Out of her chamber, led by the insane
   4. And feeble wanderings of her fading brain,
   5. The moon arose up in the murky east
   6. A white and shapeless mass.

II.
7. Art thou pale for weariness
8. Of climbing heaven and gazing on the earth,
9. Wandering companionless
10. Among the stars that have a different birth,
11. And ever changing, like a joyless eye
12. That finds no object worth its constancy?

G. **Sonnets from the Portuguese 43**, by Elizabeth Barrett Browning (1845)

1. How do I love thee? Let me count the ways.
2. I love thee to the depth and breadth and height
3. My soul can reach, when feeling out of sight
4. For the ends of Being and ideal Grace.
5. I love thee to the level of every day's
6. Most quiet need, by sun and candle-light.
7. I love thee freely, as men strive for Right;
8. I love thee purely, as they turn from Praise.
9. I love thee with the passion put to use
10. In my old griefs, and with my childhood's faith.
11. I love thee with a love I seemed to lose
12. With my lost saints—I love thee with the breath,
13. Smiles, tears, of all my life!—and, if God choose,
14. I shall but love thee better after death.

Note: There are a number of substitutions in this poem. The most difficult line is the fourth. British and American dictionaries give two pronunciations for "ideal." One treats it as a two-syllable word, the other as a three-syllable word. If you treat it as a three-syllable word, "i-dé-al," then the line scans quite simply: the first foot is read as an anapest.

H. **Explaining an Affinity for Bats**, by A. E. Stallings (1999)

1. That they are only glimpsed in silhouette,
2. And seem something else at first, a swallow,
3. And move like new tunes, difficult to follow,
4. Staggering towards an obstacle they yet
5. Avoid in a last-minute pirouette,
6. Somehow telling solid things from hollow,
7. Sounding out how high a space, or shallow,
8. Revising into deepening violet.

9. That they sing, not the way the songbird sings

10. (Whose song is rote, to ornament, finesse),
11. But travel by a sort of song that rings
12. True not in utterance, but harkenings,
13. Who find their way by calling into darkness
14. To hear their voice bounce off the shape of things.

I. **Dirge**, by Felicia Dorothea Hemans (1793—1835)

1. Calm on the bosom of thy God,
2. Fair spirit! rest thee now!
3. E'en while with ours thy footsteps trod
4. His seal was on thy brow.

5. Dust, to its narrow house beneath!
6. Soul, to its place on high!
7. They that have seen thy look in death
8. No more may fear to die!

Here are the scansions of the above poems so that you can test and confirm your scansion skills. We have not listed all the possible variations, but as we noted in the text, the first syllable in a spondee might sound to some ears as if it's unaccented. If you hear variations, ask your instructor.

A. From **The Anniad**, by Gwendolyn Brooks (1949)

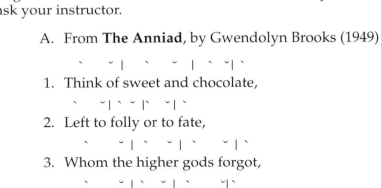

1. Think of sweet and chocolate,

2. Left to folly or to fate,

3. Whom the higher gods forgot,

4. Whom the lower gods berate;

5. Physical and underfed

6. Fancying on the featherbed

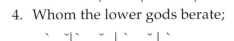

7. What was never and is not.

B. **Museum Piece**, by Richard Wilbur (1950)

˘   `   |  `   `   |˘ ` |˘ `

1. The good gray guardians of art

˘ ` | ˘  ` | ˘   ` | ˘   `

2. Patrol the halls on spongy shoes,

˘ ` | ˘  ` | ˘ ` | ˘    `

3. Impartially protective, though

˘ `  | ˘  ` | ˘   ` | ˘  `

4. Perhaps suspicious of Toulouse.

˘   ` |˘  ` | ˘ ` | ˘   `

5. Here dozes one against the wall,

˘   `  | ˘ ` | ˘ ` |˘ ˘   `

6. Disposed upon a funeral chair.

˘   ˘ |`   ` | ˘ ` | ˘ `

7. A Degas dancer pirouettes

˘ ` | ˘   ` | ˘   ` | ˘   `

8. Upon the parting of his hair.

`   ` | ˘   `  | ˘   ` |˘ `

9. See how she spins! The grace is there,

˘   `  |˘   ` |˘   ` | ˘ `

10. But strain as well is plain to see.

˘ ` | `   ˘ | `  ˘ |` ˘

11. Degas loved the two together:

`  |˘  ` | ˘ `|˘ `

12. Beauty joined to energy.

` ˘ | ˘ ` | `   ˘  |  `

13. Edgar Degas purchased once

˘ ` | ˘  ` | ˘   `  |˘  `

14. A fine El Greco, which he kept

˘ ` | ˘   ` | ˘˘ | ˘ `

15. Against the wall beside his bed

˘ ` | ˘   ` |˘ `  |˘  `

16. To hang his pants on while he slept.

C. **Juan's Song**, by Louise Bogan (1923)

```
     ˘     ` | ˘     `   | ˘    `   |˘ ` | ˘
```
1. When beauty breaks and falls asunder

```
   ˘  `  | ˘     `  | ˘  ` | ˘     `  | ˘
```
2. I feel no grief for it, but wonder.

```
      ˘    `   | ˘   ˘| `    `  | `    `| ˘
```
3. When love, like a frail shell, lies broken,

```
   ˘  `  |`    ` |˘ ` | ˘   ` | ˘
```
4. I keep no chip of it for token.

```
   ˘  ` | ˘   ` |˘    `  | ˘     `
```
5. I never had a man for friend

```
     ˘    `  |`   `  | ˘   `  | ˘    `
```
6. Who did not know that love must end.

```
   ˘  ` |˘   `  |˘ ` | ˘    `|˘
```
7. I never had a girl for lover

```
     ˘    `  | ˘  ` |  ˘   `  | ˘ `|˘
```
8. Who could discern when love was over.

```
      ˘   ˘ | `     `  | ˘    ` | ˘ `
```
9. What the wise doubt, the fool believes—

```
     `  ˘|˘   `  | ˘   `  | ˘  `
```
10. Who is it, then, that love deceives?

D. **Rondeau**, by Leigh Hunt (1838)

```
     `  ˘ | `    ˘ | `    ˘| `
```
1. Jenny kiss'd me when we met

```
      `    ˘  | `    ˘ | `   ˘ |` ˘
```
2.   Jumping from the chair she sat in;

```
    `    ˘ | `    ˘ | ` ˘| `
```
3. Time, you thief, who love to get

```
     `   ˘ |` ˘ | `  ` | ` ˘
```
4.   Sweets into your list, put that in:

```
   `   ˘ | `  ˘| `  ˘  | `
```
5. Say I'm weary, say I'm sad,

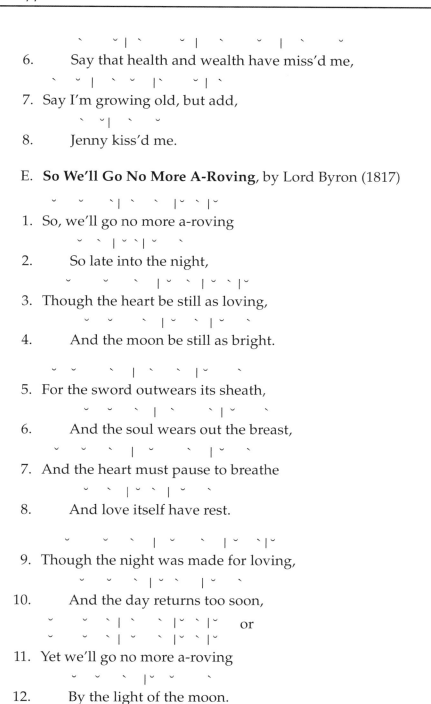

6.   Say that health and wealth have miss'd me,

7. Say I'm growing old, but add,

8.   Jenny kiss'd me.

E. **So We'll Go No More A-Roving**, by Lord Byron (1817)

1. So, we'll go no more a-roving

2.   So late into the night,

3. Though the heart be still as loving,

4.   And the moon be still as bright.

5. For the sword outwears its sheath,

6.   And the soul wears out the breast,

7. And the heart must pause to breathe

8.   And love itself have rest.

9. Though the night was made for loving,

10.   And the day returns too soon,

       or

11. Yet we'll go no more a-roving

12.   By the light of the moon.

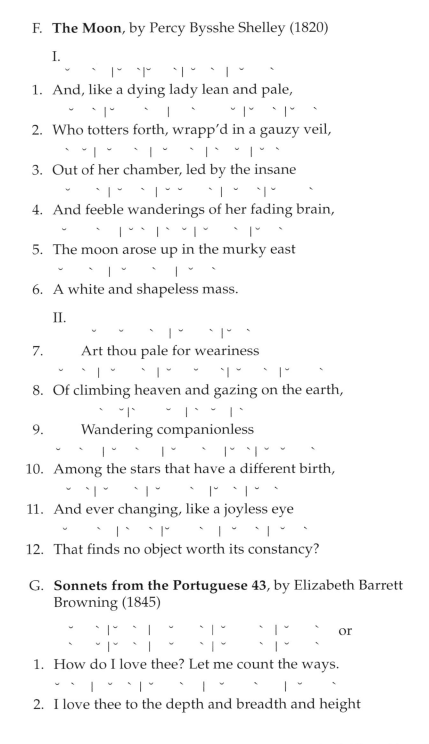

F. **The Moon**, by Percy Bysshe Shelley (1820)

   I.

1. And, like a dying lady lean and pale,

2. Who totters forth, wrapp'd in a gauzy veil,

3. Out of her chamber, led by the insane

4. And feeble wanderings of her fading brain,

5. The moon arose up in the murky east

6. A white and shapeless mass.

   II.

7.   Art thou pale for weariness

8. Of climbing heaven and gazing on the earth,

9.   Wandering companionless

10. Among the stars that have a different birth,

11. And ever changing, like a joyless eye

12. That finds no object worth its constancy?

G. **Sonnets from the Portuguese 43**, by Elizabeth Barrett Browning (1845)

                        or

1. How do I love thee? Let me count the ways.

2. I love thee to the depth and breadth and height

˘ ˋ | ˘ ˋ | ˘ ˋ |˘ ˋ |˘ ˋ

3. My soul can reach, when feeling out of sight

˘ ˘ ˋ |˘ ˋ|˘ ˋ |˘ˋ |˘ ˋ

4. For the ends of Being and ideal Grace.

˘ ˋ | ˋ ˘ | ˘ ˋ|˘ ˘ ˋ | ˘ ˋ

5. I love thee to the level of everyday's

ˋ ˋ|˘ ˋ | ˘ ˋ | ˘ ˋ | ˘ ˋ

6. Most quiet need, by sun and candle-light.

˘ ˋ | ˋ ˋ |˘ ˘| ˋ ˋ | ˘ ˋ or
˘ ˋ | ˘ ˋ |˘ ˋ| ˋ ˋ | ˘ ˋ

7. I love thee freely, as men strive for Right;

˘ ˋ | ˋ ˋ |˘ ˘| ˋ ˋ | ˘ ˋ or
˘ ˋ | ˘ ˋ |˘ ˋ| ˘ ˋ | ˘ ˋ

8. I love thee purely, as they turn from Praise.

˘ ˋ | ˋ ˘ | ˋ ˋ| ˘ ˋ | ˘ ˋ or
˘ ˋ | ˘ ˋ | ˘ ˋ| ˘ ˋ | ˘ ˋ

9. I love thee with the passion put to use

˘ ˋ | ˘ ˋ | ˘ ˋ |˘ ˋ | ˘ ˋ or
˘ ˋ | ˋ ˋ | ˘ ˋ |˘ ˋ | ˘ ˋ

10. In my old griefs, and with my childhood's faith.

˘ ˋ | ˋ ˘ |˘ ˋ |˘ ˋ | ˘ ˋ or
˘ ˋ | ˘ ˋ |˘ ˋ |˘ ˋ | ˘ ˋ

11. I love thee with a love I seemed to lose

˘ ˘| ˋ ˋ |˘ ˋ | ˘ ˋ |˘ ˋ

12. With my lost saints—I love thee with the breath,

ˋ ˋ |˘ ˋ|˘ ˋ | ˘ ˋ| ˋ ˋ or
ˋ ˋ |˘ ˋ|ˋ ˋ | ˘ ˋ| ˋ ˋ

13. Smiles, tears, of all my life!—and, if God choose,

˘ ˋ | ˘ ˋ | ˘ ˋ|˘ ˋ|˘ ˋ

14. I shall but love thee better after death.

H. Explaining an Affinity for Bats, A. E. Stallings (1999)

˘ ˋ | ˘ ˋ|˘ ˋ |˘ ˋ|˘ ˋ

1. That they are only glimpsed in silhouette,

˘ ˋ | ˋ |˘ ˋ |˘ ˋ |˘ ˋ |˘

2. And seem something else at first, a swallow,

˘   ˋ | ˘   ˋ | ˋ   ˋ | ˘ ˋ | ˘ ˋ | ˘
3. And move like new tunes, difficult to follow,

ˋ   ˘ | ˘   ˋ | ˘ ˋ | ˘ ˋ | ˘   ˋ
4. Staggering towards an obstacle they yet

˘ ˋ | ˘ ˘| ˋ   ˋ | ˘   ˋ | ˘ ˋ
5. Avoid in a last-minute pirouette,

ˋ | ˘   ˋ| ˘   ˋ| ˘ ˋ | ˘   ˋ | ˘
6. Somehow telling solid things from hollow,

ˋ | ˘   ˋ | ˘   ˋ |˘ ˋ | ˘   ˋ | ˘
7. Sounding out how high a space, or shallow,

˘   ˋ| ˘   ˋ| ˘ ˋ | ˘ ˘   ˋ| ˘ ˋ
8. Revising into deepening violet.

˘   ˘ | ˋ   ˋ | ˘   ˋ | ˘   ˋ | ˘   ˋ
9. That they sing, not the way the songbird sings

˘   ˋ | ˘ ˋ | ˘ ˋ| ˘ ˋ | ˘   ˋ
10. (Whose song is rote, to ornament, finesse),

˘   ˋ| ˘ ˋ | ˘ ˋ |˘ ˋ | ˘   ˋ
11. But travel by a sort of song that rings

ˋ   ˋ |˘ ˋ| ˘ ˋ | ˘   ˋ | ˘ ˋ
12. True not in utterance, but harkenings,

˘ ˋ | ˘   ˋ | ˘ ˋ| ˘ ˋ| ˘ ˋ | ˘
13. Who find their way by calling into darkness

˘   ˋ| ˘   ˋ | ˋ   ˋ | ˘ ˋ | ˘   ˋ
14. To hear their voice bounce off the shape of things.

I. **Dirge**, by Felicia Dorothea Hemans (1793—1835)

ˋ   ˘ | ˘   ˋ | ˘ ˋ | ˘   ˋ
1. Calm on the bosom of thy God,

ˋ   ˋ| ˘ ˋ | ˘ ˋ
2. Fair spirit! rest thee now!

˘   ˋ | ˘   ˋ | ˘ ˋ | ˘   ˋ
3. E'en while with ours thy footsteps trod

˘ ˋ | ˘ ˋ| ˘   ˋ
4. His seal was on thy brow.

5. Dust, to its narrow house beneath!

6. Soul, to its place on high!

7. They that have seen thy look in death

8. No more may fear to die!

Glossary of Poetry Terms

abstract language: Language that does not contain images (see **image**), but instead refers to concepts like love, justice, grief, virtue, reason, etc. When in *Paterson* William Carlos Williams said, "No ideas but in things," he was using abstract language to recommend using concrete images. He felt the abstractions could be implied if the details were arranged well.

accent (synonymous with *stress*): Refers to the salient monosyllabic word (see **rhetorical accent**) or a syllable in a polysyllabic word that is more prominent than others in that word. It stands out from the other surrounding syllables because it may be louder or more drawn out. The word "reward" has two syllables. The "-ward" is accented. If you say "RE-ward" rather than the "re-WARD," most speakers will think you have either mispronounced it or are using the pronunciation of the cowboy bounty hunter popularized by Hollywood. English is a strongly stressed language. As a result, we recognize two levels of stress in polysyllabic words—a primary stress and one or more secondary stresses. The primary stress is stronger (i.e., heavier, longer, or more emphatic) than the secondary stress(es). The word "uninhabited" receives its primary stress on -HAB, but the UN- receives a secondary stress. The dictionary marks it this way: un`•in•**hab**`•it•ed.

accentual poetry, accentual verse, accentuals: A type of meter in which the length of lines is governed by a consistent number of accents or stresses, but no attention is paid to the number of syllables in the line.

accentual-syllabic verse: A type of meter that depends on the pattern of accented and unaccented syllables per line.

alexandrine: A line or verse written with six iambic feet. Edmund Spenser often used a stanza in which there were eight lines of pentameter followed by an alexandrine. The term itself may have come from Old French poems about heroic figures, including Alexander the Great. The alexandrine is the most common meter in French poetry, as pentameter is in English poetry.

allegory: The Greek roots of this word mean "to speak other"; so an allegory is a work that says one thing and means another. Metaphors tend to do the same thing, but an allegory is usually an extended metaphor in which the people, actions, animals, or things are connected to things outside the narrative. George Orwell's *Animal Farm* is an allegory.

alliteration: The repetition of initial consonant sounds; however, some definitions include consonant sounds within words as well. The sentence "the wrong red ruffian was railroaded" has many alliterated "r" sounds. Note that alliteration has to do with sound, not spelling, so "wrong" would be alliterated with "red" and "ruffian." Also, the "-road" in "railroaded" could also be described as alliteration.

allusion: A brief reference to something literary, historical, religious, or cultural.

analogy: A comparison of two dissimilar things in an effort to show correspondences; metaphors and similes are analogies.

anapest: A metrical foot consisting of two unstressed syllables followed by a stress: (˘˘´).

assonance: The repetition of vowel sounds in a sequence of words.

ballad stanza: A quatrain whose first and third lines are in iambic tetrameter and whose second and fourth lines are rhymed iambic trimeter. See the sample ballad in the "Glossary of Common Poem and Stanza Forms," below.

beat: See **accent**.

blank verse: Unrhymed lines in iambic pentameter.

caesura: A break or pause in a line of poetry, usually somewhere near the middle. It is generally employed to break up the dominant rhythm, either to disguise rhyming patterns or to modulate the reading tempo. In scansion it is conventionally indicated by two parallel vertical lines: | |.

catalectic: A Greek term derived from the word *catalexis,* which literally means to "come to an abrupt end." It refers to the omission of a final syllable. In modern poetry, the most common use of the catalectic is in the omission of the final unaccented syllable in trochaic meters.

catharsis: For Plato and Aristotle, catharsis was the purgation that resulted from watching a tragic play; the audience was psychically or physically refreshed by having felt the pity and fear of the protagonist—either by identification or revulsion. Now the term has shifted to include the psychic cleansing the writer accomplishes by having written about disturbing experiences, especially among confessional poets.

complex stanza: A stanza composed of lines of different lengths. See Thomas Hardy's "Moments of Vision," pages 4–5, for an example.

conceit: A type of poetic metaphor that has an ingenious, fanciful quality; it may also form the framework for a poem or a sequence in a poem (see **extended metaphor**). John Donne's image of the compass in "A Valediction: Forbidding Mourning" is an example, as is the tent in Robert Frost's "The Silken Tent."

concrete poetry: Poetry whose meaning is primarily visual. See Mary Ellen Solt and Willis Barnstone's *Concrete Poetry: A World View* or Emmett Williams's *An Anthology of Concrete Poetry* for examples.

confessional poetry: Poetry that unabashedly and graphically examines personal difficulties; the poet speaks directly to the audience about his or her mental or physical problems. Confessional poets like Sylvia Plath,

Robert Lowell, Anne Sexton, and W. D. Snodgrass opened up new subject matter by examining the effects of alcoholism, abuse, madness, abortion, and depression; their tones were often sharper and deeper than those found in more traditional poetry. They often saw poetry as a means of achieving a personal **catharsis**, a purging of unhealthy emotions. Sylvia Plath's "Daddy" is an example of both this kind of poem and the shift in tone resulting from the catharsis experienced.

consonance: The sound echoes between the consonants in adjacent words or in rhymes. In the twentieth century it is a common rhyming strategy; word pairs like li*ve*/mo*ve*, wor*d*/lor*d*, and tor*n*/ur*n* repeat consonant sounds but are not fully rhymed. Internally, phrases like Robert Lowell's "go*bb*ets of blu*bb*er" and "iro*n*ic rai*n*bow," from "The Quaker Graveyard in Nantucket," illustrate the use of consonance as well.

couplet: A pair of lines, often rhyming. It may be a stanza or part of a poem. The last two lines of a Shakespearean sonnet, for example, are referred to as a couplet.

dactyl: A metrical foot composed of one stressed syllable followed two unstressed: (`˘˘).

diction: Choice of language. The term can be used to distinguish among kinds of language—e.g., slang, conversation, formal usage, or the specialized vocabulary of a profession.

didactic poetry: A type of poetry whose main purpose is to teach or edify. It is often written in the second person and speaks directly to the reader.

dimeter: A line of verse consisting of two metrical feet.

disyllabic meter: A meter consisting of feet made of two syllables (either iambs or trochees).

dramatic poetry: One of the three major types of poetry—**lyric**, **narrative**, and dramatic. Dramatic poetry usually has more than one character involved in some conflict. Robert Browning's "My Last Duchess" is a dramatic monologue; the Duke is speaking to the Count's emissary about his last wife and his new proposal.

elision: Leaving out or slurring over (from the verb *elide*). In speech, we often compress a three-syllable word into two; occasionally, poets will count on this compression in the scansion of their poems. Words like "family," "dalliance," or "ivory" will often be scanned as if they had only two syllables. Poets prior to the twentieth century often used elisions to make their meters smoother; common elisions included words like o'er (over), e'en (even), 'mid (amid), or 'twas (it was). These elisions changed two syllables into one.

end-stopped: A line with a pause at its end, one with some sense of grammatical completion. Heavily end-stopped lines conclude with periods or semicolons. The effect of end-stopped lines is to make each line, as a unit, stand out.

enjambment: The continuation of line that runs over into the next one without any pause at its end. It is the opposite of an end-stopping. Two lines are enjambed when you must read the second to comprehend the first.

envoi / envoy: Literally, "to send away" or one who is sent away. Originally, the envoi was a postscript dedicating the poem to a patron or prince. It now refers to a short concluding stanza at the end of certain French verse forms. It often concludes through a pattern of repetition or rhyme. For example, the sestina concludes with an envoi that repeats all six end words in a tercet rather than the sestets that make up the rest of the poem.

epigraph: A quotation at the beginning of a book, chapter, or poem.

expectation pattern: The pattern that repetition of a meter builds in the reader. After being exposed to a metrical poem for a few lines, the reader tends to expect the pattern to continue and may even anticipate it.

explication: A method of writing about poems whereby one looks carefully at the metaphors, ambiguities, interrelationships, and sonic effects of the language in the poem. C. Hugh Holman and William Harmon, in their *Handbook to Literature,* suggest that this term is derived from *explication de texte,* a French method of analysis, which "originated in the teaching of literature in France."

extended metaphor: A metaphor that is detailed and developed into a network of associations; it can be extended over several lines or for the length of the poem. Robert Frost's "The Silken Tent" is an example of a poem-length extension; John Donne's compass image at the end of "A Valediction: Forbidding Mourning" is extended over the last three quatrains.

falling rhyme: An rhyme that ends with an unaccented syllable; for example, "maybe" and "baby." Occasionally there may even be a second unaccented syllable, as in "hastily"/"tastily." A rhyme that ends with the last syllable stressed is called a **rising rhyme** (as in "delay" and "convey"). The old terms that marked this distinction were *feminine* and *masculine* rhymes.

falling rhythm: A foot that ends on an unaccented syllable.

feet: See **foot**.

figurative language: Language that uses figures of speech, which include metaphors, similes, irony, paradox, metonymy, synecdoche, and apostrophe. Therefore, it is language that deviates from conventional meaning, syntax, or significance. The term is most commonly used to indicate any metaphoric usage in the broadest sense.

figures of speech: See **figurative language.**

fixed form: A poem whose length and rules of line length and meter are defined. The sonnet, villanelle, and sestina are fixed forms.

foot: The basic unit of rhythm in poetry. A line of formal poetry consists of a specific number of feet. The most common feet are iambs, trochees, anapests, dactyls, and spondees.

free verse: Poetry written without predictable meter; often meter and rhyme are used in free verse, but not in a consistent pattern.

function words: Words like prepositions (*to, for, at*) and conjunctions (*and, or, but*) that convey less meaning in a sentence than nouns and verbs, and are thus less likely to get a rhetorical stress. They may receive a metrical stress.

hemistich: A half line of poetry usually divided by spacing; it was a common division in Old English, especially in accentual and alliterative Anglo-Saxon poetry.

heptameter: A line of poetry consisting of seven feet.

heroic couplet: A rhymed couplet that is usually end-stopped and in iambic pentameter. Alexander Pope used this measure frequently in his poetry, and John Dryden used it in several of his plays.

hexameter: A line of poetry consisting of six feet. In Greek, it was the conventional meter for epic and didactic poetry, and its pattern was a specific interplay of dactyls, spondees, and trochees.

hypermetric: A line that has an extra syllable or foot that is not part of the regular pattern.

hypometric: A line that lacks syllables or feet and is not thus consistent with the regular pattern.

iamb: A metrical foot consisting of one unaccented syllable followed by an accented one (˘´).

image: The terms *image* and *imagery* are widely used but definitions are complex and varied. An image can be contained in a metaphor, a simile, a figure of speech, a symbol, an extended metaphor, or a sensory descriptive word or phrase. It may even refer to the impression left in the mind of the reader or viewer. It has been argued that the term is so vague that it ought not be used; however, we use it to refer simply to a phrase or word that makes reference to what can be sensed—what can be seen, smelled, felt, heard, or tasted. A simile can convey an image— "skies of couple-color as a brinded cow"; and any sensory word can convey a less complicated image as well. The word "tree" presents an image. So does "bitter." The word "good" does not.

imagery: The concrete objects and sensory experiences used to convey meaning. Imagery is not just decorative; it conveys levels of meaning that can be both personally and more generally referential.

irony: A figure of speech in which what is said is not what is meant. It has a variety of forms. Irony is like sarcasm, but it is usually less harsh. It often refers to knowledge held by the audience but not shared by the characters or some literary predecessor. If a critic said, "In Williams's yard is a red wheelbarrow glazed with rhetoric," he would be expressing an oblique criticism of William Carlos Williams's minimalist experiment with clarity and objectivity. The remark appears to be innocent, but it contains a subterranean message that depends upon prior knowledge—a knowledge of Williams's poem and what he was trying to do in it. This critic thinks that even the minimalist has a rhetorical agenda.

lexical stress: In a line of poetry, this is an accent in a word with more than one syllable, a polysyllabic word. These accents or stresses can be found in a dictionary. For example, the word "lexical" is accented on the first syllable (see page 16 for a more complete definition).

line: The basic unit of metrical verse. Except for prose poems, all poems are written in lines. In metrical verse the line break is determined by the line's metrical length. It is metered using one of several schemes discussed in this book. Also see **verse**.

literal language: Language that is not **figurative**. If we said the car was "hot," its literal meaning suggests a high temperature; its figurative meaning suggests its potential for speed, its appearance, or its popularity. Literal language is denotative while figurative language is connotative. If we say that a translation is literal, we mean that there has been no real attempt to convey nuances of tone, meaning, or style.

lyric poetry: A term derived from "lyre" that indicates a short, emotional song that once would have been accompanied on a lyre, a stringed instrument like a small harp. Now it is generally regarded as one of three types of poems: the lyric, **narrative**, and **dramatic**. The lyric poem is usually short, musical, and about the emotions of the speaker. Shakespeare's sonnets are examples.

meditative poetry: A term that was applied to the English metaphysical poetry of the sixteenth and seventeenth centuries; these poems tended to be about faith and religious issues. Today, the term is more loosely applied by critics like Robert Pinsky and Jonathan Holden to any poem whose primary concerns are about the relationship of ideas to one's life. Wallace Stevens's "Sunday Morning" is an example.

metaphor: An associative comparison between two phenomena used to illustrate their similarities or differences. When John Keats calls his Grecian urn a "sylvan historian," he wants to emphasize its value as a recorder of our ancient pastoral past.

meter: The rhythmic pattern used in verse. There are four kinds of meter: (1) quantitative, the meter most often used in classical poetry, in which the rhythm is established by patterns of long and short syllables; (2) accentual, in which the occurrence of stressed or accented syllables establishes the basic line regardless of the number of unstressed syllables around them; (3) syllabic, in which the number of syllables in each line determines its length rather than its pattern of stressed and unstressed syllables; and (4) accentual-syllabic, in which the number of accents is fixed and the number of unstressed syllables is also usually consistent. When we use the word "meter" in English, we are typically referring to accentual-syllabic poetry.

metrical accent / metrical stress: A stress that occurs on a weak syllable in a line of poetry because an existing pattern of stresses forces one there. If the line were not in a poem such an accent would not be heard. A metrical accent is most often found on a function word or the weak syllable of a polysyllabic word (its secondary accent). For example, in a word like "environment" the primary stress, and thus lexical stress, is on "-vi," but in an iambic line there would be a metrical stress on "-ment" as well (see pages 16–17 for a more complete definition).

mixed metaphor: This is a combination of two metaphors that do not function well together. Some mixed metaphors are used deliberately for comic effect, but most are inadvertently comic. They are often created by using two clichés without visualizing them together. Sentences like "We were all in the same boat until someone pulled the rug out from under us," "He's a dyed-in-the-wool lame duck," or "In my neck of the woods you'd better know the ropes" are examples. Even Shakespeare's mixed metaphor in Hamlet's soliloquy is somewhat comic: "to take arms against a sea of troubles and by opposing end them" (ending up with a rusty sword is more likely).

monologue: A poem spoken by one character. There are two kinds of monologue—*internal* and *dramatic*. An internal monologue conveys the thoughts of the poem's speaker, much like a soliloquy in which a character addresses the audience of a play directly. Hamlet's famous "To be or not to be" speech is an example of this "thinking out loud." A dramatic monologue, however, suggests that the speaker is actually addressing another person. Robert Browning's "Soliloquy of the Spanish Cloister" is an internal monologue because the monk is speaking to himself; Browning's "My Last Duchess" is a dramatic monologue because the Duke is speaking to the Count's emissary.

monometer: A line of poetry containing one foot; it is an uncommon meter except in stanzas whose line lengths vary.

monosyllabic foot: A one-syllable foot consisting of a single accent: (`).

narrative poetry: One of the three major types of poems—**lyric,** narrative, and **dramatic**. A narrative poem, such as an epic, a ballad, or a romance, tells a story. "Sir Patrick Spens" is a ballad that tells the story of a knight who is sent to his death at sea.

octameter: A line of poetry consisting of eight feet.

octave / octet: Generally, the first eight lines of an Italian sonnet; the last six lines are called the **sestet**. The rhyme scheme is *abbaabba*. The term can loosely refer to any group of eight lines. *Octave* refers to an eight-line stanza but can also be used as a synonym for octet.

onomatopoeia: Refers to the imitation of natural sounds by words. The word illustrates its meaning. For example, "woosh" could be used to describe the sound of wind. Words can be onomatopoetic in degrees; it is a somewhat subjective term. For example, we often use "bow-wow" to describe the bark of a dog, but it is only partly onomatopoetic because different breeds of dog make different sounds and different cultures hear the sounds differently; Russians, for example, hear the same barking as "guff guff." Words like "slap," "pop," "slam," "whistle," "splat," "buzz," "bang," and "bristle" are attempts to illustrate sounds.

parody: The deliberate mocking of a serious composition by imitating its style or tone. Anthony Hecht's "Dover Bitch" is a parody of Matthew Arnold's "Dover Beach"; however, as Charles Colton once noted, "Imitation is the sincerest flattery," and these parodies often come out of respect for the original.

pastoral: A term derived from *pastor,* Latin for "shepherd." A pastoral poem or play is about the simple rustic life of shepherds; it is usually a deliberately naïve wish for an escape from the demands and complications of an urban life. Greek and Roman poets wrote pastorals, and this convention was revived during the Renaissance. Modern pastoral poems often extol the simplicities of bucolic life, regardless of their actual acquaintance with it.

pentameter: A metrical line consisting of five feet.

persona poem: A poem told from the first-person point of view but whose speaker is not identified with the poet. Persona literally means "mask," and the writer is putting on a mask for the duration of the poem. Poets can write from the perspective of historical figures, different genders, other poets, even animate or inanimate objects. In this book, W. B. Yeats's "An Irish Airman Foresees His Death" and Joseph Powell's "Mirrors" are examples.

personification: A **figure of speech** that gives ideas, abstractions, animals, or things human characteristics. Robert Herrick's "a careless shoestring" is an example.

prose poem: A poem printed in paragraphs like prose rather than set up in lines and stanzas.

prosody: The study of poetic meters, rhythms, forms, and structures.

pyrrhic: A metrical foot of two unaccented syllables: (˘˘). Many critics have argued that pyrrhics do not exist in English; we maintain that they only appear as part of a super-iamb, a fused compound foot: two unaccented syllables followed by a spondee. Prosodists who spot them regularly generally find unaccented syllables where we find **metrical stresses**.

quantitative verse: Verse in which the measuring unit is based on combinations of vowel length. The terms for accentual-syllabic feet come from Greek and Latin poetry, where their meaning was slightly different because these languages employ quantitative verse. In Latin poetry an *iamb* is a short syllable followed by a long syllable, rather than an unaccented syllable followed by an accented syllable. Attempts have been made to employ quantitative verse in English. See "A Note on Sapphics," pages 78–80.

quatrain: A stanza or poem of four lines; a poem may be written in four-line stanzas, or a quatrain may be included as a variation in a poem with stanzas having different lengths.

reversed foot: A metrical variation in which the dominant foot is replaced by its mirror image. Thus, a trochee is a reversed foot in an iambic line, and a dactyl is a reversed foot in an anapestic line.

rhetorical accent, rhetorical stress: One sort of stress we assign to monosyllabic words in a metered line. Rhetorical accents fall on words that would be emphasized in a prose reading because they convey important information. This emphasis is contextual (see page 16 for a more complete discussion).

rhyme: An inclusive term for syllables that "echo" each other. There are several terms distinguishing the degree to which the rhyme words mimic each other. There is *full rhyme,* where the last syllable or a monosyllable has a full sonic echo. For example, "wait"/"fate" and "weather"/"together" are full rhymes. We also identify rhyme that is *slant* or merely echoes a full rhyme; more precise ears like to make finer distinctions and identify 3/4, 1/2, and 1/4 rhyme. A rhyme like "beautiful"/"school" might be 3/4, and "windowpane" / "pen" might be 1/2, and "bodiless"/ "promise" might be 1/4; however, we feel these distinctions are too fine for our purposes and that *slant* suffices to indicate rhymes that are anything less than full. Furthermore, "less" does not imply a value judgment; because English is a rhyme-poor language, poets in the twentieth century have used slant rhyme to keep the language more surprising and submerge the technical elements so that they aren't so obvious. We also refer to *internal rhyme:* rhymes that echo within or between lines. We distinguish these from *end rhyme.*

rhyme scheme: The pattern of rhymes in a poem or stanza. It can be described by using letters from the beginning of the alphabet for rhyming words, one letter for each rhyme sound. In a four-line stanza in which the first and fourth lines rhyme with each other, and the second and third lines rhyme with each other, the rhyme scheme is designated *abba*—the two *a*'s are lines 1 and 4; the two *b*'s lines are 2 and 3. The letters *x* and/or *y* are often used to indicate lines that do not rhyme. So if only the second and fourth lines of a stanza rhymed, the rhyme scheme could be described as *xaxa*.

rising rhyme: An end rhyme on an accented syllable; for example, "beside" and "confide" are rising rhymes. The old term was *masculine rhyme*. **Falling rhymes** have their accents on the next-to-last syllable, as in "maybe" and "baby." The old term for falling rhyme was *feminine rhyme*.

rising rhythm: A metrical foot that ends on an accented syllable.

scan: To perform a **scansion**.

scansion: A complete metrical description of a line or poem, using symbols to indicate stressed syllables, unstressed syllables, and how they are organized into feet. When a poem is scanned, the accents are usually indicated with ` marks; the unaccented syllables are indicated with ˘ marks. The feet are then marked off with virgules (|) or clearly delineated with spacing. It is important not to forget this last step. If feet are not indicated, the person reading the scansion will not know what the basic foot is nor how many there are to a line. Furthermore, the reader needs to be able to see where and for what reasons variations have occurred.

sestet: An Italian sonnet is often broken into two parts: an eight-line stanza or **octet** and a six-line stanza or sestet. The rhyme scheme of the sestet is usually *cdecde*. The term *sestet* can technically refer to any six-line stanza or poem.

simile: A figure of speech in which two things are being compared; most similes are introduced with *like* or *as*. The comparisons are generally of dissimilar things, yet they share some quality or property. When Thomas Hardy writes that "the swallows flew . . . like little crossbows," he is suggesting that swallows and crossbows share a visual similarity.

skeltonics: Lines of two or three stresses whose end rhyme usually repeats in couplets but can go on for three or four lines.

speaker: Although the speaker in a poem may be the poet himself or herself, it is conventional to assume that a poem's narrator is not necessarily the poet. Sometimes the speaker is very much a character the poet has invented, as in the case of Robert Browning's "My Last Duchess," whose Duke is the speaker.

spondee: A metrical foot having two accented syllables: ("").

stanza: The grouping of lines in a poem, similar to the paragraph in prose. In formal poems, the stanzas generally have the same number of lines, line length, rhyme scheme, and metrical form. Typical stanza lengths include the couplet, tercet, quatrain, quintet, sestet, septet, and octet or octave.

stress: See **accent**.

substitution: Also called a *variation*, the term refers to the substitution of one metrical foot for another; for example, if the poet is writing in iambic pentameter, then uses a trochee, spondee, anapest, or dactyl in place of one of the five iambs called for by a line of iambic pentameter, that trochee, spondee, anapest, or dactyl is called a substitution.

super-iamb: A double foot in which a pyrrhic (˘˘) and a spondee (``) are fused and occur as ˘ ˘ | ` ` . This line from William Wordsworth's "Lines" (better known as "Tintern Abbey") is an example:

˘ ˘ | `   `|˘   `  | ˘   ` |˘   `

of the deep rivers and the lonely streams.

See W. B. Yeats's "Adam's Curse" for several other examples.

syllabic poetry, syllabic verse, syllabics: A type of poetry in which line length is determined by the number of syllables. Because it has no prevailing rhythm or sound effect, it is a form that can appear to be somewhat arbitrary, but the poems of Marianne Moore, Kenneth Rexroth, and John Hollander are effective exceptions.

symbol: A symbol combines a literal quality with abstract or suggestive possibilities. Some symbols have an inherent acquired meaning; for example, a road suggests a journey or the path of life, and the dark suggests uncertainty, death, ignorance, or the unknown. Other symbols depend on their context, like William Blake's tyger, Edgar Allan Poe's raven, or Robert Frost's silken tent.

synecdoche: A figure of speech in which a part signifies the whole. Henry Wadsworth Longfellow's "Such an old mustache am I" is an example.

synesthesia: A combination of two sense impressions; for example, "a green sound," "a loud jacket," "sweet discord," would all illustrate this crossover of the senses. It was a common characteristic in the Symbolist poetry of Charles Baudelaire and Arthur Rimbaud.

tetrameter: A metrical line consisting of four feet.

tone: The attitude of the speaker toward the subject of the poem. We use this term in speech; when your mother says "Don't use that tone with me, young lady," she is objecting to your attitude, which was probably sarcastic or superior. The tone of a **lyric poem** can be sad, wistful, angry, ironic, sarcastic, tender, joyous, etc. If you mistake the tone of an **ironic** poem for sincerity, you could miss the idea of the poem entirely, so it is important to be attuned to tonal clues.

trimeter: A line consisting of three feet.

trisyllabic meter: A meter whose basic foot consists of three syllables—either dactyls or anapests.

trochee: A metrical foot consisting of two syllables, an accented syllable followed by an unaccented syllable.

unaccented syllable: A syllable that does not receive a stress or accent in a line of poetry.

variation: A metrical foot that deviates from the one used as the prevailing meter of the poem. Thus, if a poem is written in an iambic meter, the substitution of a trochee, spondee, anapest, or dactyl for one of the iambs would be a variation. A variation can also refer to a deviation from a standard form; poets have written sestinas with four sestets instead of six.

verse: A group of lines or a section in a metrical poem. It can also be used as a generic term to distinguish between poetry and prose. In that case *verse* means poetry written in lines. In free verse, there is no fixed measure. In metrical verse, line length is determined by a consistent measuring scheme such as in accentual-syllabic verse.

virgule: A vertical— | —or slanted—/—slash used to mark foot boundaries or line breaks.

Glossary of Fixed Forms and Stanza Forms

haiku: A Japanese syllabic poem whose three lines have a five-seven-five syllable pattern. Haiku usually make some reference to a season. However, modern haiku often disregard these requirements and use strong images without much abstraction or didacticism. The haiku depends on juxtaposition and suggestion to make its connections and statements.

> The haybailer rumbles
> over the windrowed field:
> I read the newspaper.

limerick: Light verse that is often bawdy or nonsensical. The form is five lines of accentual-syllabic verse rhyming *aabba*; the first, second, and fifth lines have three feet and the third and fourth have two. The rhythm is usually anapestic. It may have originated in Limerick, but some scholars suggest it was brought to this Irish town in the early eighteenth century by returning veterans of the French war.

> On my way to the annual dance
> I split out the seat of my pants.
>   Miss Molly McGuire
>   had the nerve to inquire
> about the odd look of my stance.

pantoum: Originally a Malay form, it is written in quatrains, and the second and fourth lines of one stanza must appear as the first and third lines of the following stanza. In the final stanza, the first and third lines of the first stanza must recur in reverse order—the poem then ends with the same line with which it began. The rhyme scheme for each stanza is usually *abab*. Peter Meinke's "Atomic Pantoum" is a particularly fine example; however, he chose not to have it rhyme.

> In a chain reaction
> the neutrons released
> split other nuclei
> which release more neutrons
>
> The neutrons released
> blow open some others
> which released more neutrons
> and start this all over
>
> Blow open some others
> and choirs will crumble

and start this all over
with eyes burned to ashes

And choirs will crumble
the fish catch on fire
with eyes burned to ashes
in a chain reaction

The fish catch on fire
because the sun's force
in a chain reaction
has blazed in our minds

Because the sun's force
with plutonium trigger
has blazed in our minds
we are dying to use it

With plutonium trigger
curled and tightened
we are dying to use it
torching our enemies

Curled and tightened
blind to the end
torching our enemies
we sing to Jesus

Blind to the end
split up like nuclei
we sing to Jesus
in a chain reaction

rondeau: A French form consisting of fifteen lines; the ninth and fifteenth are a short refrain taken from the first few feet of the first line. It was derived from a dance song, and the refrain was sung by the chorus. Generally, there are only two rhymes in the entire poem; the refrain lines are not part of the rhyme scheme, which is *aabba aabx aabbax*. Typically, the poem is written in iambic tetrameter or pentameter. Here is an example by Paul Laurence Dunbar called "We Wear the Mask":

We wear the mask that grins and lies,
It hides our cheeks and shades our eyes, —
This debt we pay to human guile;
With torn and bleeding hearts we smile,
And mouth with myriad subtleties.

Why should the world be over-wise,
In counting all our tears and sighs?
Nay, let them only see us, while
We wear the mask.

We smile, but, O great Christ, our cries
To thee from tortured souls arise.
We sing, but oh the clay is vile
Beneath our feet, and long the mile;
But let the world dream otherwise,
We wear the mask!

sestina: A complicated verse form that came to us through the French trouba-
dour poets. It has six sestets with an envoy of three lines. The English
versions of this poem often had lines of ten syllables; however, in mod-
ern sestinas the line length is rarely consistent. The poem has a complex
system of repeating words. If we number the words that end the initial
stanza, then we can see how the end words repeat: 1-2-3-4-5-6; 6-1-5-2-
4-3; 3-6-4-1-2-5; 5-3-2-6-1-4; 4-5-1-3-6-2; 2-4-6-5-3-1. The three lines of the
envoy generally end in a 5-3-1, which repeats the last three end-words
of the last sestet. The remaining end words, 2-4-6, are worked some-
where into the interior of these three lines, so that all six words are re-
peated in the envoy. Modern poets have varied the pattern of the end-
words in the envoy; the following sestina by Mark Halperin, "Mists and
Imagined Fields," ends in a 5-1-6, and the interior pattern is 4-2-3. Some
early versions used rhyme in the sestets.

As an eye sweeps the horizon's stubby mountains,
graying, layered blues, a wedge of lake
glinting between the tall buildings and fields
of orange roofs, how easy to imagine
this is the day we arrived: fallen leaves
and snow, the renewed green and a welcome mist.

That snaps the heat spell. A fine mist,
floating rather than falling, swathes the mountains,
serpentine as memory. We will leave
ghostlike flames behind to dance on the lake
at evening, grit to burnish it. Imagine,
clean each morning, the waiting, misty fields

scented like fresh sheets. They are paddies, not fields
though. We want only what is, like mist,
so fleeting yet full it could not be imagined:
lashed bamboo drying racks, mountains
of pine feathers, and sunsets on the lake
burned into our dreams although we leave

by intricate paths and gates. Before we leave,
the arches of the bridges should echo the field
of weeds in a graveyard taking the wind, the lake's
every curving inlet. We should have missed
nothing. But to the west, past the mountains,
is a town with fish in the streets. Who could imagine

the yellow and orange dots on their backs? Imagine
missing that. Is there time before we leave
for everything: camping in the mountains?
street festivals? the sky a field
of fireflowers, booming with blooming mists
that hang a few seconds above the lake

in puzzled brilliance? When we are gone, the lake
will return to darkness and quiet. We can imagine
all that follows as unimportant. What is missed
is lost. Familiar faces, the day we leave,
might shine from frozen photographs, from fields—
and part of us remain in the eyes of mountains.

Trying to imagine our return, did we leave
ourselves stranded by lakes in those mountains,
waving from their bridges, dissolving like fields of mist?

sonnet: Typically a fourteen-line poem, written in iambic pentameter, and rhymed. Many modern poets have called poems sonnets that are neither metered nor rhymed; their only relation to the sonnet is the number of lines and even that has been challenged by some poets. The sonnet traditionally referred to two particular types—the Italian (also called Petrarchan) or the English (also called Shakespearean). Both were fourteen lines, in iambic pentameter, and rhymed. The poem is often divided into two parts, an octave and a sestet. The Italian sonnet's octave is rhymed *abbaabba* and the sestet *cdecde* or *cdcdcd* or *cdedce*. The English sonnet rhymes *ababcdcd efefgg*. Edmund Spenser is also credited with a particular sonnet form; he used three quatrains and a couplet whose rhyme scheme was *abab bcbc cdcd ee*. Here is an example (130) from Shakespeare's sonnet sequence:

My mistress' eyes are nothing like the sun;
Coral is far more red than her lips' red;
If snow be white, why then her breasts are dun;
If hairs be wires, black wires grow on her head.
I have seen roses damasked, red and white,
But no such roses see I in her cheeks;
And in some perfumes is there more delight
Than in the breath that from my mistress reeks.
I love to hear her speak, yet well I know
That music hath a far more pleasing sound;
I grant I never saw a goddess go;
My mistress, when she walks, treads on the ground.
And yet, by heaven, I think my love as rare
As any she belied with false compare.

triolet: A French form that consists of eight lines. The French use syllabics, but versions in English are accentual-syllabic. Line lengths may vary. The first two lines are repeated as the last two. The first line is also repeated in the fourth line. There are only two rhymes, and the rhyme scheme is *abaaabab*. Contemporary triolets include Sandra McPherson's "Triolet," Harold Witt's "First Photo of Flu Virus," and Barbara Howes's "Early Supper." Here is an example from Thomas Hardy, "At a Hasty Wedding":

If hours be years the twain are blest,
For now they solace swift desire
By bonds of every bond the best,
If hours be years. The twain are blest
Do eastern slopes never west,
Nor pallid ashes follow fire:
If hours be years the twain are blest,
For now they solace swift desire.

villanelle: A complicated French form of nineteen lines with only two rhyme sounds, and the repetition of whole lines in an alternating pattern. The first line is repeated in lines 6, 12, and 18; the third line is repeated in lines 9, 15, and 19. Notice that the first and third lines are brought together at the end as lines 18 and 19. The villanelle is written in tercets with a quatrain at the end, and the rhyme scheme is *aba aba aba aba aba* and *abaa*. It is often written in iambic pentameter, but some modern variations have abandoned this requirement. Three of the finest villanelles written in English are Dylan Thomas's "Do Not Go Gentle into That Good Night," Theodore Roethke's "The Waking," and Elizabeth Bishop's "One Art" (see page 84).

Glossary of Common Poem and Stanza Forms

aubade: A morning song that has dawn as its setting; it is usually in praise of the new day, about the regrets of parting lovers or time's advances. Here is an example from John Donne called "The Sun Rising."

> Busy old fool, unruly sun,
> Why dost thou thus,
> Through windows, and through curtains call on us?
> Must to thy motions lovers' seasons run?
> Saucy pedantic wretch, go chide
> Late schoolboys and sour prentices,
> Go tell court-huntsmen that the king will ride,
> Call country ants to harvest offices;
> Love, all alike, no season knows nor clime,
> Nor hours, days, months, which are the rags of time.
>
> Thy beams, so reverend and strong
> Why shouldst thou think?
> I could eclipse and cloud them with a wink,
> But that I would not lose her sight so long;
> If her eyes have not blinded thine,
> Look, and tomorrow late, tell me,
> Whether both the Indias of spice and mine
> Be where thou left'st them, or lie here with me.
> Ask for those kings whom thou saw'st yesterday,
> And thou shalt hear, All here in one bed lay.
>
> She's all states, all princes, I,
> Nothing else is.
> Princes do but play us; compared to this,
> All honor's mimic, all wealth alchemy.
> Thou, sun, art half as happy as we,
> In that the world's contracted thus;
> Thine age asks ease, and since thy duties be
> To warm the world, that's done in warming us.
> Shine here to us, and thou art everywhere;
> This bed thy center is, these walls, thy sphere.

ballad: A short narrative poem often characterized by oblique questions and dialogue; it is accentual/syllabic and is written in quatrains rhymed *xaxa,* where the first and third lines are in iambic tetrameter and the second and fourth are in trimeter. It is derived from the oral tradition, and many are written to be sung. It is an old form, dating back at least to the four-

teenth century, whose history and original form are under debate. The
"Ballad of Birmingham" is a modern one written by Dudley Randall
about the bombing of a church in Birmingham, Alabama, during the
civil rights struggle in 1963:

"Mother dear, may I go downtown
Instead of out to play,
And march the streets of Birmingham
In a Freedom March today?"

"No, baby, no, you may not go,
For the dogs are fierce and wild,
And clubs and hoses, guns and jails
Aren't good for a little child."

"But, mother, I won't be alone.
Other children will go with me,
And march the streets of Birmingham
To make our country free."

"No, baby, no, you may not go,
For I fear those guns will fire.
But you may go to church instead
And sing in the children's choir."

She has combed and brushed her night-dark hair,
And bathed rose petal sweet.
And drawn white gloves on her small brown hands,
And white shoes on her feet.

The mother smiled to know her child
Was in the sacred place,
But that smile was the last smile
To come upon her face.

For when she heard the explosion,
Her eyes grew wet and wild.
She raced through the streets of Birmingham
Calling for her child.

She clawed through bits of glass and brick,
Then lifted out a shoe.
"Oh, here's the shoe my baby wore,
But, baby, where are you?"

common meter: Like the ballad stanza, a form that uses quatrains, which are
composed of alternating lines of iambic tetrameter and trimeter. The
major difference is in the rhyme scheme: the ballad is typically *xaxa*, and
common meter is *abab*. This is the form common to hymnals, and these
songs are often designated with a *C.M.* This form was often used by
Emily Dickinson.

elegy: A meditation on death, usually occasioned by the death of a particular person. Perhaps the most famous elegy in English is Thomas Gray's "Elegy Written in a Country Churchyard," in which the speaker considers the lives of illiterate country people who may have had great potential but never had the chance to fulfill it. While a "eulogy" literally means "good words" said about the dead, an elegy can be satirical or ironic, although it is usually a poem that praises the character or some attribute of the dead. The following elegy, in which a scholar speaks to his dead wife, was written in ninth-century China by Yuan Chen and translated by Sam Hamill; it is titled "Elegy."

> O loveliest daughter of Hsieh,
> you married a hapless scholar
> and spent your life with a sewing basket,
> patching his old clothes.
>
> He thanked you
> by selling your gold hairpins for wine;
> he picked you herbs and berries
> for your dinner
> and locust leaves for the fire.
>
> Now that they pay me handsomely
> there's no offering I can bring
> but this sacrificial mourning.
> We used to joke about dying.
>
> And now you are suddenly gone.
> I gave all your clothes away
> and packed your needlework—
> I couldn't bear to see them.
>
> But I continue your kindness toward our maid,
> and sometimes bring you gifts in my lonely dreams.
> Everyone learns this sorrow, but none
> more than those who suffer together.
>
> Alone and lonely, I mourn us both.
> Almost seventy, I know better men
> who lived without a son, better poets
> with dead wives who couldn't hear them.
>
> In the dark of your tomb,
> there is nothing left to hope for—
> we had no faith in meeting after death.
> Yet when I open my sleepless eyes,
>
> I see through those long nights,
> the grief that troubled your life.

epic: A long narrative poem that usually describes the exploits of heroic people important to a nation's or race's origins. Its style is elevated. The Babylonian tale called *Gilgamesh* was an oral poem in the epic tradition;

Homer's *Iliad*, Virgil's *Aeneid*, and John Milton's *Paradise Lost* are Western examples of great epics.

epigram: A concise saying that could be inscribed on monuments, buildings, or gravestones. At least since Martial, a Roman epigrammist, the epigram has been seen as a short, witty, satirical poem. The tone is generally light, and the poems may be about a variety of subjects. Epigrams are usually written in couplets or quatrains. The poetry of Alexander Pope has been called epigrammatic because so many of his couplets seem detachable and worthy of quotation. Here is a sample adapted from Martial:

Once a surgeon, Dr. Baker,
Then became an undertaker,
Not so much his trade reversing
Since for him it's just re-hearsing. (Lind 1957, 264)

epithalamium: A Greek term that literally means "at the bridal chamber" and refers to poems written for or about weddings, like this poem by Joseph Powell, simply called "Epithalamion."

Crickets have quit
scratching away the dark
and the sun comes up arguing,
involving everything it touches
like a spoiled child.
Because it was this day
the clock inside you chose to marry,
you can't sleep
and watch the sun push down the mountains,
inflame the mist over the river.
Fear overtakes all you see,
doubt blossoming.

Like a premonition that happened
you have believed feeling's mystery
but hesitate at the thought
of standing before so many,
reciting words as old as love,
that each day require new definitions.
The chastened child in you
suspects happiness,
thinks it lives beyond us
in a blue illusion
like those distant mountains
just now coming into view.

But there are whole moments
outside yourself, when you walk
along the river as full of the world
as your pockets with things to bring home,

or when scaly rooftops suddenly
seemed perched for flight.

The kitchen rattles its dishes
and the house that wandered all night
comes back to stand in its usual place.
You dress in separate rooms,
move toward what's left to be done
and the day the house hid begins,
a door closing, a mist disappearing.

free verse: A poem that does not have a consistent metrical pattern.

ghazal: A Persian form in which there is only one rhyme (*aa ba ca,* etc.), and the typical subject is love, though the tone is usually one of melancholy or sadness. Arabic, Persian, Turkish, and Urdu poets often mention their names toward the end of the poem. Some modern American poets have taken liberties with this form; they seem attracted to the narrative leaps from stanza to stanza, its nervous energy. Here is a good example by Michael Collier, called "Ghazal."

When I was young I couldn't wait to leave home
and then I went away to make the world my home.

In England a poet's wife suggested a word for what I felt,
"heimweh." German for homesickness even when you're home.

The agoraphobe and claustrophobe respectively
cannot bear to leave or stay inside their home.

Our day-old son wrapped in a blanket in your arms
and I'm in the car waiting to take both of you home.

Mortgage means "dead pledge." To buy a house
you need one. A house can be mistaken for a home.

It won't be hard to name the poet who wrote a sonnet sequence
about his mother and father. He called it "The Broken Home."

A shovel, rake, and pickax hang inside my neighbor's garage.
Like a god he has ordered the chaos of his home.

Never let me forget: colliers mine coal. Michael's an angel.
In heaven as on earth the coal of grief warms the soul's home.

ode: Originally a Greek form used in dramatic poetry and accompanied by music. It had three movements: strophe, antistrophe, and epode. In the tragedy, the chorus would consider one point of view from one side of the stage, consider the opposite point of view from the other side, and come to some conclusion at center stage. The internal form of the ode often retains this structure. The formal ode is usually accentual-syllabic and rhymed. Its tone is serious, elevated, dignified. Pindar's odes often commemorated an Olympic athletic achievement or a military success. John Keats wrote odes to a nightingale, melancholy, a Grecian urn, and

Psyche. Modern odes in free verse tend to work against the formality and seriousness of the ancient odes. Pablo Neruda's "Ode to My Socks" and William Stafford's "Ode to Garlic" celebrate the commonplace by using elevated diction to describe mundane things.

ottava rima: A **stanza** of eight iambic pentameter lines rhymed *ababab cc*. Boccaccio has been credited with originating the stanza. Sir Philip Sidney used it in "Old Arcadia," John Milton in the coda of "Lycidas," and George Gordon, Lord Byron in "Don Juan." Great modern examples are W. B. Yeats's "Among School Children" and "Sailing to Byzantium."

paean: A lyric poem that was a song of praise or joy. In Greek poetry it was a song addressed to Apollo, a god of healing, beauty, and truth. It was sung on several occasions: commencing battle, returning victorious, at the beginning of symposia, or greeting victorious generals. Today, the term refers to poems of unreserved praise.

Spenserian stanza: The stanza Edmund Spenser used in *The Faerie Queene*. It is composed of nine lines, and the first eight are in iambic pentameter. The last one is an alexandrine or in iambic hexameter. The rhyme scheme is *ababbcbcc*. John Keats used this stanza form in "The Eve of St. Agnes"; Percy Bysshe Shelley used it in "The Revolt of Islam." It is an uncommon stanza form in contemporary poetry.

terza rima: As the name implies, it is an Italian form. It is accentual-syllabic, written in three-line stanzas whose rhymes interlock; the rhyme scheme is *aba bcb cdc ded,* etc. It is usually written in iambic pentameter. The last stanza closes in a variety of ways—a couplet, a quatrain, or tercet—but there is usually an attempt to tie off the last unrhymed end word with a double or triple rhyme. Dante Alighieri's *Divine Comedy*, Percy Bysshe Shelley's "Ode to the West Wind," and George Gordon, Lord Byron's "Prophecy of Dante" are examples. Modern examples include Robert Frost's "Acquainted with the Night" and W. H. Auden's "The Sea and the Mirror." Here is Frost's "Acquainted with the Night":

I have been one acquainted with the night.
I have walked out in rain—and back in rain.
I have outwalked the furthest city light.

I have looked down the saddest city lane.
I have passed by the watchman on his beat
And dropped my eyes, unwilling to explain.

I have stood still and stopped the sound of feet
When far away an interrupted cry
Came over houses from another street,

But not to call me back or say good-bye;
And further still at an unearthly height,
One luminary clock against the sky

Proclaimed the time is neither wrong nor right.
I have been one acquainted with the night.

Works Cited

Attridge, Derek. 1982. *Rhythms of English Poetry*. New York: Longman.

Auden, W. H. 1976. *Collected Poems*, ed. Edward Mendelson. New York: Random House.

Barzun, Jacques. 2000. *From Dawn to Decadence: 1500 to the Present; Five Hundred Years of Western Cultural Life*. New York: HarperCollins.

Bishop, Elizabeth. 1969. *The Complete Poems*. New York: Farrar, Straus and Giroux.

Blake, William. 1965. *The Poetry and Prose of William Blake*, ed. David V. Erdman. New York: Doubleday.

Bogan, Louise. 1977. *The Blue Estuaries: Poems, 1923–1968*. New York: Ecco.

Brooks, Gwendolyn. 1963. *Selected Poems*. New York: Harper and Row.

Browning, Elizabeth. 1977. *Sonnets from the Portuguese,* ed. William S. Peterson. Barre, MA: Barre.

Byron, George Gordon. 1977. *Selected Poems and Letters*, ed. William H. Marshall. New York: New York University Press.

Celce-Murcia, Marianne, and Diane Larsen-Freeman. 1999. *The Grammar Book: An ESL/EFL Teacher's Course*, 2d ed., with Howard Williams. Boston: Heinle and Heinle.

Clare, John. 1970. "Come Hither." Pp. 680–81 in *The Norton Anthology of Poetry*, ed. Arthur M. Eastman, et al. New York: Norton.

Collier, Michael. 2000. *The Ledge*. New York: Houghton Mifflin.

Cullen, Countee. 1991. *My Soul's High Song: The Collected Writings of Countee Cullen, Voice of the Harlem Renaissance*, ed. Gerald Early. New York: Doubleday.

Dickinson, Emily. 1960. *The Complete Poems of Emily Dickinson*, ed. Thomas H. Johnson. Boston: Little, Brown.

Donne, John. 1968. *The Complete Poetry of John Donne*, ed. John T. Shawcross. New York: New York University Press.

Dromgoole, Will Allen. 1974. "Old Ladies." P. 133 in Nims 1974.

Dunbar, Paul Laurence. 1913. *The Complete Poems of Paul Laurence Dunbar*. New York: Dodd, Mead.

Frost, Robert. 1969. *The Poetry of Robert Frost*, ed. Edward Connery Lathem. New York: Holt, Rinehart and Winston.

———. 1995. "The Figure a Poem Makes." Pp. 776–78 in *Collected Poems, Prose, and Plays*. New York: Library of America.

Fussell, Paul. 1979. *Poetic Meter and Poetic Form*, rev. ed. New York: Random House.

Gray, David. 1878. "My Little Brother." Pp. 962–63 in *The Family Library of British Poetry from Chaucer to the Present Time (1350–1878)*, ed. James T. Fields and Edwin P. Whipple. Cambridge: Riverside.

Gunn, Thom. 1995. *Collected Poems*. New York: Noonday Press / Farrar, Straus and Giroux.

Halperin, Mark. 1976. "The Alarm." P. 65 in *Backroads*. Pittsburgh: University of Pittsburgh Press; London: Feffer and Simons. 1976.

———. "Resolve." P. 68 in *Backroads*. Pittsburgh: University of Pittsburgh Press; London: Feffer and Simons.

———. 1990. "Mists and Imagined Fields." Pp. 64–65 in *The Measure of Islands*. Middletown, CT: Wesleyan University Press.

Hardy, Thomas. 1898. "The Temporary the All." Pp. 1–3 in *Wessex Poems and Other Verses*. New York and London: Harper and Brothers.

———. 1901. "At a Hasty Wedding." P. 148 in *Poems of the Past and the Present*. New York and London: Harper and Brothers.

———. 1914. "Wessex Heights." Pp. 32–34 in *Satires of Circumstance: Lyrics and Reveries with Miscellaneous Pieces*. London: Macmillan.

———. 1917. "Moments of Vision." P. 1 in *Moments of Vision and Miscellaneous Verses*. London: Macmillan.

Hemans, Felicia Dorothea. 1878. "Dirge." P. 840 in *The Family Library of British Poetry from Chaucer to the Present Time (1350–1878)*, ed. James T. Fields and Edwin P. Whipple. Cambridge: Riverside.

Herrick, Robert. 1968. *The Complete Poetry of Robert Herrick*, ed. J. Max Patrick. New York: Norton.

Holden, Jonathan. 1986. *Style and Authenticity in Postmodern Poetry*. Columbia: University of Missouri Press.

Holman, C. Hugh, and William Harmon. 1992. *A Handbook to Literature,* 6th ed. New York: Macmillan.

Hood, Thomas. 1970. *Selected Poems of Thomas Hood*, ed. John Clubbe. Cambridge, MA: Harvard University Press.

Hopkins, Gerard Manley. 1986. *Gerard Manley Hopkins*, ed. Catherine Phillips. New York: Oxford University Press.

Housman, A. E. 1932. *A Shropshire Lad*. New York: Hartsdale House.

Hunt, Leigh. 1978. *The Poetical Works of Leigh Hunt*, ed. H. S. Milford. New York: AMS Press.

Joyce, James. 1967. *Collected Poems*. New York: Viking.

———. 1968. *Dubliners*. New York: Viking.

Keats, John. 1959. *Selected Poems and Letters*, ed. Douglas Bush. Boston: Houghton Mifflin.

Kennedy, X. J. *Literature: An Introduction to Fiction, Poetry, and Drama*. Boston: Little, Brown, 1976.

Kingsley, Charles. 1943. "The Sands of Dee." P. 87 in *A Treasury of the Familiar*, ed. Ralph Woods. New York: Macmillan.

Knox, Bernard. 1990. Introd. to *The Iliad*, by Homer, trans. Robert Fagles. New York: Viking.

Lawrence, D. H. 1964. *The Complete Poems*, ed. Vivian de Sola Pinto and F. Warren Roberts. New York: Viking.

Lind, L. R. 1957. *Latin Poetry in Verse Translation, from the Beginnings to the Renaissance.* Boston: Houghton Mifflin.

Lowell, Robert. 1992. *Selected Poems,* rev. ed. New York: Noonday Press / Farrar, Straus and Giroux.

Marvell, Andrew. 1966. *The Complete Works, Vol. 1: Verse*, ed. Alexander B. Grosart. New York: AMS Press.

McKay, Claude. 1973. *The Passion of Claude McKay: Selected Poetry and Prose, 1912–1948*, ed. Wayne F. Cooper. New York: Schocken.

McKuen, Rod. 1967. *Listen to the Warm*. New York: Random House.

———. 1966. *Stanyan Street and Other Sorrows*. New York: Random House.

Meinke, Peter. 1991. *Liquid Paper: New and Selected Poems*. Pittsburgh: University of Pittsburgh Press.

Mitcham, Judson. 2003. *This April Day*. Tallahassee: Anhinga.

Mueller, Lisel. 1996. *Alive Together: New and Selected Poems*. Baton Rouge: Louisiana State University Press.

Nims, John Frederick. 1974. *Western Wind*: *An Introduction to Poetry*. New York: Random House.

Omond, T. S. 1903/1968. *English Metrists: Being a Sketch of English Prosodical Criticism from Elizabethan Times to the Present Day*. New York: Phaeton.

Parry, Milman. 1971. *The Making of Homeric Verse: The Collected Papers of Milman Parry,* ed. Adam Parry. Oxford: Clarendon Press.

Pinsky, Robert. 1978. *The Situation of Poetry: Contemporary Poetry and Its Traditions*. Princeton, NJ: Princeton University Press.

Pope, Alexander. 1963. *The Poems of Alexander Pope: A One-Volume Edition of the Twickenham Text with Selected Annotations*, ed. John Butt. New Haven: Yale University Press.

Powell, Joseph. 1986. "Epithalamion." P. 57 in *Counting the Change*. Pp. 1–62 in *QRL Poetry Series 7*, vol. 26. Princeton, NJ: Quarterly Review of Literature.

———. 1993a. "If, Love." P. 21 in *Winter Insomnia*. Corvallis, OR: Arrowood Books.

———. 1993b. "Mirrors." P. 36–38 in *Getting Here*. Pp. 1–59 in *QRL Poetry Book Series,* vol. 36. Princeton, NJ: Quarterly Review of Literature.

Preminger, Alex, and T. V. F. Brogan. 1993. *The New Princeton Encyclopedia of Poetry and Poetics*. Princeton, NJ: Princeton University Press.

Randall, Dudley. 1968. *Cities Burning*. Detroit: Broadside.

Rich, Adrienne. 1984. *The Fact of a Doorframe: Poems Selected and New, 1950–1984*. New York: Norton.

Roethke, Theodore. 1966. *The Collected Poems of Theodore Roethke*. New York: Doubleday.

Shelley, Percy Bysshe. 1963. *Selected Poetry and Prose*, ed. Kenneth Neill Cameron. New York: Holt, Rinehart and Winston.

Solt, Mary Ellen, and Willis Barnstone. 1969. *Concrete Poetry: A World View*. Bloomington: Indiana University Press.

Stallings, A. E. 1999. "Explaining an Affinity for Bats." *Formalist* 10.2: 34.

———. 2002. "Étude." *Formalist* 13.2: 41.

Taylor, Jane. 1942. "My Mother." Pp. 506–07 in *A Treasury of the Familiar*, ed. Ralph Woods. New York: Macmillan.

Thomas, Edward. 1978. *The Collected Poems of Edward Thomas*, ed. R. George Thomas. Oxford: Clarendon Press.

Whitman, Walt. 2002. *Leaves of Grass and Other Writings*, ed. Michael Moon. New York: Norton.

Wilbur, Richard. 1989. *New and Collected Poems*. San Diego: Harcourt Brace Jovanovich.

Williams, Emmett. 1967. *An Anthology of Concrete Poetry*. New York: Something Else Press.

Williams, William Carlos. 1963. *Paterson*. New York: New Directions, 1963.

———. 1989. *The Collected Poems of William Carlos Williams*. Vol. 2, *1939–1962*, ed. Christopher MacGowan. New York: New Directions Books.

Wood, Clement. 1940. *Poets' Handbook*. New York: Greenberg.

Wyatt, Thomas. 1969. *Collected Poems of Sir Thomas Wyatt*, ed. Kenneth Muir and Patricia Thomson. Liverpool: Liverpool University Press.

Yeats, W. B. 1989. *The Collected Works of W. B. Yeats*. Vol. 1, *The Poems*, ed. Richard J. Finneran. New York: Macmillan.

Yuan Chen. 2000. "Elegy." Pp. 191–92 in *Crossing the Yellow River: Three Hundred Poems from the Chinese*, trans. Sam Hamill. New York: BOA Editions.

Index

Authors

Mark Halperin is emeritus professor of English at Central Washington University, where he taught for thirty-six years and was named 2002 Distinguished Professor in Creativity. He was a Fulbright Scholar to Moscow, Russia, and returned there to teach as a visiting professor, as well as teaching at Shimane University, Japan. His publications include four books of poetry, *Backroads*, *A Place Made Fast*, *The Measure of Islands*, and *Time as Distance*, as well as a number of chapbooks. His poems have appeared in such magazines as *Poetry*, the *Yale Review*, *Prairie Schooner*, and the *Seattle Review*. He has also published translations from contemporary Russian poets, fiction writers, and essayists.

Joseph Powell is professor of English at Central Washington University, and has taught introduction to poetry and poetry writing classes for over twenty years. He has also taught as an exchange professor at universities in Greece and Hungary. His publications include three full-length collections of poetry: *Counting the Change* (1986), *Getting Here* (1993), and *Winter Insomnia* (1993), and three chapbooks: *Aegean Dialogues* (1998), *Greatest Hits: 1980–2001* (2001), and *A Ring in Air* (2003). He has published poems in over sixty magazines and newspapers, including *Poetry*, the *Nebraska Review*, the *Southern Poetry Review*, the *Seattle Review*, the *Christian Science Monitor*, the *Seattle Times*, and *Tar River Poetry*.

This book was typeset in Palatino and Helvetica by Electronic Imaging.
The typeface used on the cover was Univers.
The book was printed on 60-lb. Accent Opaque Offset paper by Versa Press.